Jesus Christ Visited Ancient America

by

Almon Fackrell

DORRANCE PUBLISHING CO., INC.
PITTSBURGH, PENNSYLVANIA 15222

Dorrance Publishing Co., Inc.
701 Smithfield Street
Pittsburgh, PA 15222
Visit our website at *www.dorrancebookstore.com*

ISBN: 978-1-4349-2869-6
eISBN: 978-1-4349-2221-2

About the Cover

In The Blue Circle:
The Israelite Savior
Moses' Serpent on a Pole

"And the LORD said unto Moses, Make thee a fiery *serpent*, and set it upon a pole: and it shall come to pass, that every one that is bitten, when he looketh upon it, shall live. And Moses made a *serpent* of brass, and put it upon a pole, and it came to pass, that if a serpent had bitten any man, *when he beheld the serpent of brass, he lived*."

Numbers 21:8-9

In The Red Circle:
The Christian Savior
Jesus Christ on the Cross

Shown is: *The Crucifixion* by Carl Heinrich Bloch (1834-1890) located in the Frederiksborg Museum at Hillerod, Denmark.

"And as Moses lifted up the *serpent* in the wilderness, even so must the *Son of man (Jesus)* be lifted up: that whosoever believeth in him should not perish, but have *eternal* life."

John 3:14-15

Yes—Moses' serpent on a pole was a prophetic symbol of Jesus Christ on the cross. The Israelites were saved from their afflictions by looking upon their serpent savior, and all mankind may be saved eternally by looking upon the Christian Savior, Jesus Christ.

In The Green Circle:
The Ancient American Savior
Quetzalcoatl Carrying His Cross

"The Aztecs have a tradition of a god suffering and crucified named Quetzalcoatl" (Kingsborough, *Antiquities of Mexico*, Vol. 8, p.3,1848).

The *Codex Fejervary-Mayer,* an ancient manuscript, shows the bearded god of the Pochtecas carrying his cross. The Pochtecas were a brotherhood of merchants who traveled as missionaries to spread the gospel of Quetzalcoatl, the "feathered serpent," and sell their goods for their sustenance. They were treated like royalty.

The descriptive name of this god was Yacatecmhtli, which means "Lord of the Vanguard." There are four reasons why many believe this is another of the many names of Quetzalcoatl, (See 4.13 herein).

1) He is called "Lord"—Only Quetzalcoatl and Yacatecuhtli, among all the gods was preeminently called "Lord" (See 4.48 herein).
2) He has a beard—Only Quetzalcoatl and Yacatecuhtli have beards in all the history of ancient America. Most male descendants of the ancient Americans do not have beards.
3) His Vanguard—missionaries—taught the gospel of Quetzalcoatl.
4) Quetzalcoatl was crucified, thus the cross is one of his most important symbols (See Kingsborough, *Antiquities of Mexico,* Vol. 8, p. 3).
   Yes—The "Lord of the Vanguard" was Quetzalcoatl.

Introduction

In the spring of 1981, my wife and I celebrated our twenty-fifth wedding anniversary by flying down into Mexico to visit some ancient ruins of the Aztec and Mayan Indians.

First, we visited the Aztec Temples and Pyramids at Teotihuacan, just a few miles north of Mexico City, and we were really impressed with the pyramid upon which the Temple of Quetzalcoatl used to be. We were told that Quetzalcoatl was a bearded white god who visited ancient America about 2000 years ago.

Then we flew over to Merida, Yucatan, and visited the Mayan ruins at Chichen Itza. The most interesting building in this ancient city was El Castillo, or The Castle. On top of this pyramid is the Temple of Kukulkan. I climbed up to the temple, and there at the entrance was a carved image of Kukulkan—a man with a beard.

Since this trip, I have been obsessed with gathering information about Quetzalcoatl and Kukulkan. Both names mean "feathered serpent." And they both represent a white man-god with a beard who visited America about 2000 years ago.

I kept thinking that the only white man-god with a beard that I am acquainted with was Jesus in the New Testament who lived about 2000 years ago. Could it be that Quetzalcoatl and Kukulkan were none other than Jesus Christ? Did Jesus come over to the people of ancient America and teach them his gospel after his resurrection?

Jesus is the God of the whole world. His gospel should be preached to all people in all parts of the world. Even gentiles, non-Israelites, were taught the gospel after the resurrection of Christ.

Jesus told his Apostles, "Go ye therefore, and teach all nations..." (Matthew 28:19).

Yes—Good people all over the world should have the opportunity to hear, learn, and accept the true word of God, especially if they are part of the Holy Tribes of Israel. And we know that during New Testament times, the twelve tribes of Israel were scattered abroad.

> "James a servant of God and of the Lord Jesus Christ, to the twelve tribes which are scattered abroad, Greetings" (James 1:1).

What about Jesus? Did he go and teach those other tribes of Israel outside of the Holy Land? After his resurrection, he visited the Israelites in and around Jerusalem for forty days, teaching them his gospel.

> "To whom also HE showed himself alive after his passion by many infallible proofs, being seen of them forty days, and speaking of the things pertaining to the kingdom of God" (Acts 1:3).

Did Jesus go and show himself to any of the other tribes of Israel scattered abroad? Yes, he did. He said this to his disciples:

> "I am the good shepherd, and know my sheep, and am known of mine...And *other sheep I have*, which are *not of this fold:* them also I must bring, and *they shall hear my voice...*" (John 10:14-16).

Yes—Jesus knows his chosen Israelites, and he knows where they are. And he said they would hear his voice.

Were there Israelites in ancient America when they were scattered abroad? And did Jesus come over, visit, and teach them? This is a theory that has some super strong evidences.

This study is a collection of historical, scriptural, traditional, and mythological data arranged in a manner to show the similar characteristics that exist between the ancient Americans and the Israelites, between the ancient Americans and the Christians; also, the parallels between Quetzalcoatl and Jesus Christ, and between Tezcatlipoca, the evil god of the ancient Americans, and Satan, the evil god of the Bible.

The main objective is to show the possibility that Quetzalcoatl and Jesus Christ are one and the same person.

There are many people who will never accept these theories. In opposition to this study—I have already received three major objections:

Objection No. 1- The religions of the ancient Americans were full of abominable practices such as human sacrifices, honoring man gods, worshiping the sun, moon, stars, wind, rain, etc., which are contrary to the teachings of both the Old and New Testaments.

Objection No. 2- The symbol and name of Quetzalcoatl, the American counterpart of Jesus, indicates "serpent," and since the serpent is considered by many people to be the symbol of the devil, he could not be connected with the true God and the prophets. Thus, he must have been an evil being, inspired by Satan.

Objection No. 3- Only those traditions and myths which support this study have been chosen to show the evidences that Israelite and Christian practices were in ancient America and that Jesus and Quetzalcoatl might be one and the same person.

What about Objection Number One?

The practices of cutting out beating hearts upon sacrificial altars with obsidian knives, throwing beautiful young maidens and infants into sacred wells, and worshiping the sun, moon and stars, are just about the extent of knowledge most people have of religion in ancient America. What they do not know is that this type of worship replaced a once highly civilized religion believed and practiced just a couple of centuries before the coming of the Spaniards.

Quetzalcoatl taught about love and mercy. He could not bear to hurt any living animal, let alone the sacrifice of human beings; his sacrifices were of fruits and flowers; very different from the religion which existed when the Spaniards arrived in America (See 4.68 herein.).

It was Tezcatlipoca, the Satan of ancient America, who originated the evil doctrines of human sacrifice (See the following: Nicholson, *Mexican and Central American Mythology,* pp. 10-70; Brundage, *The Fifth Sun,* pp. 114 and 208, and Burland and Forman, *The Aztecs,* p. 71).

What about Objection Number Two?

Most people relate the *serpent* with things evil and devilish. Even modern dictionaries define it with such words as "treacherous," "malicious," "crafty," "sly," etc. But, the truth of the matter is that even through it is a biblical symbol of Satan, based on the Garden of Eden story, the serpent is also a biblical symbol of Christ on the cross! "Blasphemy!" some say? Well, let's see.

The Apostle John teaches us:

> "As Moses lifted up the *serpent* in the wilderness, even so must
> the *Son of man* be lifted up, that whosoever believeth in him
> should not perish, but have eternal life" (John 3:14-15).

Yes—the serpent lifted up by Moses represented the future Lord Jesus Christ being lifted up on the cross.

The story of the serpent lifted up by Moses is in reference to when the Israelites were being bitten by fiery serpents in the wilderness after their exodus from Egypt. It was the Lord who instructed Moses to make a brass fiery serpent and put it upon a pole, and if the bitten Israelites would look upon the brass serpent, with faith, they would live (See Numbers 21:6-9). And similarly, those who would look upon the Christian *serpent* on the pole would live eternally. So, for the Christians, the serpent savior of the Israelites was a type and a symbol of their own "Savior serpent" who was also hung upon a pole.

It is very surprising that it is the medical profession that uses the serpent on the pole, with feathers, as their symbol of being the healers, and not the Christians. But I know that it wouldn't be right to use a serpent as a symbol of Christ.

In addition to the brass serpent of Moses, there are also other *good* serpents in the Bible. In Exodus 4:2-5, the Lord caused Moses' rod to become a serpent to demonstrate that God's power was with him. Then in Exodus 7:9-12, Aaron's rod became a serpent that destroyed the serpents of the Egyptian magicians.

These examples of good serpents having more power than bad serpents were indicating the future fulfillment of God's prophesy in Genesis 3:15, which indicates that the "devil-serpent" has power to bruise the heel of the seed of Eve, but the "Christ-serpent" has power to bruise the devil serpent's head, an interpretation that is common among some Christian theologians.

Maybe it was more than just a coincidence that Jesus told his disciples to be *feathered serpents*, when he said:

> "...be ye therefore wise as serpents and harmless as doves" (Matthew 10:16).

Did Jesus mean be wise like the Devil? I don't think so.

So, even though some people believe there is no such thing as a good serpent; just as there are poisonous and non-poisonous snakes, there is a good serpent and it is a symbol of the Messiah, and the bad serpent is a symbol of the adversary. As pointed out in this study, Quetzalcoatl was a good feathered-serpent.

What about Objection Number Three?

Yes—only those traditions and myths which support this study have been chosen to show the evidences that Jesus and Quetzalcoatl are the same person, and that Israelite and Christian practices were in ancient America.

I admit the fact that there are some references which are contrary to what this study is trying to prove. For example, while most sources say that Quetzalcoatl's hair was light colored, there are a couple references that indicate that his hair was black. Another example is when Quetzalcoatl was tempted; a few traditions say that the results of this temptation were failure, whereas we know that Jesus was sinless.

The theory behind this study is not an open and shut case. The major defense against this objection is that myths and traditions are very imperfect, and especially after the Ancient Americans had discarded Quetzalcoatl as their main god in favor of Tezcatlipoca, the god of evil, just a couple of centuries before the Spaniards arrived.

The facts were greatly distorted by apostate people under the influence of their Lucifer, Tezcatlipoca (See Section Five).

The support for this study far outnumbers those which do not.

Contents

Section One

Israelites
Were in
Ancient America

Why would Jesus visit ancient America?
Because there were Israelites in Ancient America. Jesus himself said:

> "...I am not sent but unto the *lost sheep* of the House of Israel" (Matthew 15:24).

The theory that some of the American-Indians are Israelites is not new. Here are the titles of three very wonderful books which testify to the truthfulness of this theory: *Jews in America,* published in 1650 by Reverend Thomas Thorowgood; *View of the Hebrews: or the Tribes of Israel in America,* published in 1825 by Reverend Ethan Smith and; *Indians or Jews?,* published in 1973 by Lynn Glaser.

Soon after the discovery of America and meeting its natives, this theory has been expressed and several writers, both Christian and Jewish, acknowledged that there were Israelites in the Americas.

One Jewish writer was Manasseh ben Israel who wrote his book, *The Hope of Israel,* published in 1652. He explained that in the city of Gaming, Peru, there was a large building that was made by bearded, white people who arrived there long before the Spaniards.

He suspected they were Israelites of the lost ten tribes and he further explained:

> "...he that will compare the Laws and Customs of the Indians and Hebrews together, shall find them agree in many things" (Manasseh ben Israel, *The Hope of Israel,* p. 22).

So let us compare the American Indians with the Hebrew Israelites.

1.1   THE ISRAELITES BELIEVED IN MORE THAN ONE GOD, BUT THERE WAS ONE SUPREME GOD.

The *Godhead*, also known as the *Trinity*, has three members: the Father, the Son and the Holy Ghost. The Father is the most high God. "...Blessed be Abram of *the most high God*, possessor of heaven and earth" (Genesis 14:19).

"And they fell upon their faces, and said, O *god the God of the spirits of all flesh...*" (Numbers 16:22).

SOME ANCIENT AMERICANS BELIEVED IN MORE THAN ONE GOD, BUT THERE WAS ONE SUPREME GOD.

The Trinity doctrine is found in the *Popol Vuh,* which is a very sacred book of the Mayan Indians (See 2.4 herein). The Aztecs recognized the existence of a supreme creator and Lord of the universe. They addressed him in their prayers as "God by whom we live, omnipresent, that knoweth all thoughts, and giveth all gifts without whom a man is as nothing, invisible, incorporeal, one God, of perfect perfection and purity" (Prescott. *History of the Conquest of Mexico,* Vol. 1, p. 78).

The Aztecs spoke about Ometeo the great god, above all (See Nicholson. *Mexican and Central American Mythology,* p. 114-115).

1.2   THERE WAS A SPIRIT CREATION OF ALL THINGS BEFORE THE PHYSICAL CREATION, ACCORDING TO THE ISRAELITES.

Genesis chapter one records the creation of plants, animals, and man. Then Genesis 2:4-7 says: "These are the generations of the heavens and of the earth when they were created.... And every plant of the field before it was in the earth, and every herb of the field before it grew...and there was not a man to till the ground...And the LORD God formed man of the dust of the ground and breathed into his nostrils the breath of life; and man became a living soul."

When the earth was created: "...all the sons of God shouted for joy" (Job 38:7). Thus, all the sons of God existed as spirits before the earth was created.

"Before I formed thee in the belly I knew thee; and before thou camest forth out of the womb I sanctified thee, and I ordained thee a prophet unto the nations" (Jeremiah 1:5).

THERE WAS A SPIRIT CREATION OF ALL THINGS BEFORE THE PHYSICAL CREATION, ACCORDING TO SOME ANCIENT AMERICANS;

"Together with time, space is thus given a special and miraculous significance. Like the *first time* outside material creation, there must have been a *first space.* Indeed the two concepts cannot be separated" (Nicholson. *Mexican and Central American Mythology,* p. 21).

1.3   LUCIFER, THE DEVIL OF THE ISRAELITES, WAS "CAST OUT OF HEAVEN."

"How art thou fallen from heaven, O Lucifer, son of the morning...For thou hast said in thine heart, I will ascend into heaven, I will exalt my throne above the stars of God...I will be like the most High" (Isaiah 14:12-14).

TEZCATLIPOCA, THE DEVIL OF SOME ANCIENT AMERICANS, WAS "CAST OUT OF HEAVEN."

Many writers say Tezcatlipoca fell from heaven, and others say seven devils called "satai," came from heaven (Brundage. *The Fifth* Sun, p. 94, also see p. 95; Makemson. *The Book of the Jaguar Priest,* p. 35; Nicholson. *Mexican and Central American Mythology,* pp. 98 and 109).

Satan was in ancient America (See Section Five herein.).

1.4   THE ISRAELITES BELIEVED THEY HAD A PRE-MORTAL LIFE BEFORE THEY WERE BORN ON EARTH.

When a person dies..."Then shall the dust return to the earth as it was: and the spirit shall return unto God who gave it" (Ecclesiastes 12:7).

The Lord said to Jeremiah: "Before I formed thee in the belly I knew thee; and before thou camest forth out of the womb I sanctified thee, and I ordained thee a prophet unto the nations" (Jeremiah 1:4-5).

SOME ANCIENT AMERICANS BELIEVED THEY HAD A PRE-MORTAL LIFE BEFORE THEY WERE BORN ON EARTH.

The gods in heaven sent children down to earth to be born.

Ancient Americans talked about a "first space," or the "first time" outside material creation (Brundage. *The Fifth Sun,* p. 54; Nicholson. *Mexican and Central American Mythology,* p. 21).

1.5   THE STORY OF THE "TREE OF LIFE" IS DESCRIBED BY THE ISRAELITES.

"And the LORD God said, Behold, the man is become as one of us, to know good and evil: and now, lest he put forth his hand, and take also of the tree of life, and eat, and live for ever...So he drove out the man; and he placed at the east of the garden of Eden Cherubims, and a flaming sword which turned every way, to keep the way of the tree of life" (Genesis 3:22-24).

THE STORY OF THE "TREE OF LIFE" IS DESCRIBED BY THE ANCIENT AMERICANS.

Many writers of ancient America describe the "tree of life" as a "sacred tree" and a "tree of the fountain of life" (Bancroft. *History of Mexico,* Vol. 2, p. 182; Burland. C.A. *The Gods of Mexico,* p. 176; Nicholson. *Mexican and Central American Mythology,* p. 22; Toor. *A Treasury of*

Mexican Folkways, p. 104; Von Hagen. *The Ancient Sun Kingdoms of the Americas,* photo no. XLIX, after p. 490).

1.6   A STORY OF A FORBIDDEN TREE IS TOLD BY THE ISRAELITES.

"And unto Adam he said, Because thou hast…eaten of the tree, of which I commanded thee, saying, Thou shalt not eat of it: cursed is the ground for thy sake; in sorrow shalt thou eat of it all the days of thy life…In the sweat of thy face shalt thou eat bread, till thou return unto the ground…" (Genesis 3:17-19).

A STORY OF A FORBIDDEN TREE IS TOLD BY SOME ANCIENT AMERICANS.

The *Popol Vuh,* the sacred book of the ancient Quiche Maya of the highlands of Guatemala, tells us a lot about this forbidden tree (See 1.7 below and 2.18-2.20 herein.).

Several writings of the ancient Americans tell about this tree (Roys. *The Book of Chilam Balam of Chumayel,* p. 119).

1.7   ISRAELITES TAUGHT THAT A WOMAN WAS THE FIRST TO TOUCH THE FORBIDDEN TREE.

"And the LORD God said unto the woman, What is this that thou hast done? And the woman said, The serpent beguiled me, and I did eat…Unto the woman he said, I will greatly multiply thy sorrow…" (Genesis 3:13, 16).

SOME ANCIENT AMERICANS TAUGHT THAT A WOMAN WAS THE FIRST TO TOUCH THE FORBIDDEN TREE.

"Ah!' she exclaimed, 'What fruit is this which this tree bears? Is it not wonderful to see how it is covered with fruit? Must I die, shall I be lost, if I pick one of this fruit?' said the maiden" (Goetz and Morley, *Popol Vuh,* p. 119; Brundage. *The Fifth Sun,* p. 161; see also p. 46).

1.8   SOME ISRAELITES TELL ABOUT THE GREAT FLOOD THAT COVERED THE EARTH.

"And the rain was upon the earth forty days and forty nights.

In the selfsame day entered Noah, and Shem, and Ham, and Japheth, the sons of Noah, and Noah's wife, and three wives of his sons with them, into the ark…And the waters prevailed exceedingly upon the earth; and all the high hills, that were under the whole heaven, were covered" (Genesis 7:12-19).

THE AZTECS, INCAS, AND MAYANS KNEW ABOUT THE GREAT FLOOD THAT COVERED THE EARTH.

(These references are in addition to the one mentioned in the Popol Vuh—See 2.19 herein.)

"Further, the new rites and doctrines—of the Spaniards—had many similarities to their own...the flood—of Noah—existed in recorded traditions" (Bancroft. *History of Mexico,* Vol. 2, p. 182).

There are many ancient American traditions about when the sky collapsed, when earth people were killed by a flood, and the universal "water-over-the-earth" (Brundage. *The Fifth Sun,* pp. 6 and 47; Guidoni and Magni. *The Andes,* p. 10.7; Nicholson. *Mexican and Central American Mythology,* p. 56; Von Hagen. *The Ancient Sun Kingdoms of the Americas,* p. 352).

1.9   SOME ISRAELITES TELL ABOUT NOAH AND HIS FAMILY WHO SURVIVED THE GREAT FLOOD THAT COVERED THE EARTH.

"Make thee an ark of gopher wood; rooms shalt thou make in the ark, and shalt pitch it within and without with pitch...And of every living thing of all flesh, two of every sort shalt thou bring into the ark, to keep them alive with thee: they shall be male and female" (Genesis 6:14-19).

"...*Noah* only remained alive, and they that were with him in the *ark*" (Genesis 7:23).

NOAH WAS KNOWN AS "TAPI" BY THE MAYANS AND "NOTA" BY THE AZTECS.

Mayans: "...a god-fearing man called *Tapi*...to whom one day the god revealed himself and gave a very strange commandment...to *build a ship*, and should take on to it his wife and all his possessions and *two* of every kind of beast. Tapi steered his ship...let out all his beasts and became the father of mankind" (Honore. *In Quest of the White God,* p. 33).

Aztecs: Nota and Nona, were saved from the great deluge (Toor. *A Treasury of Mexican Folkways,* pp. 458-459).

1.10   THE BIBLICAL STORY OF THE FLOOD TELLS OF A DOVE THAT WAS SENT OUT TO FIND LAND AND NEVER RETURNED.

"... Noah opened the window of the ark which he had made...he sent forth a dove from him, to see if the waters were abated from off the face of the ground; But the dove found no rest for the sole of her foot, and she returned unto him into the ark, for the waters were on the face of the whole earth...And he stayed yet another seven days; and again he sent forth the dove out of the ark; And the dove came in to him in the evening; and, lo, in her mouth was an olive leaf plucked off: so Noah knew that the waters were abated from off the earth. And he stayed yet other seven days; and sent forth the dove; which returned not again unto him anymore" (Genesis 8:6-12).

THE AZTEC LEGEND OF THE FLOOD TELLS OF A DOVE THAT WAS SENT OUT TO FIND LAND AND NEVER RETURNED.

"At last the rain stopped...Tapi sent out a dove. It flew off, but did not return, for it had found land" (Honore. *In Quest of the White God*, p. 33).

1.11 THE ISRAELITES DESCRIBE THE RAINBOW AS A SYMBOL OF THE COVENANT TO STOP RAIN.

"And God spake unto Noah...saying...I will establish my covenant with you; neither shall all flesh be cut off any more by the waters of a flood; neither shall there any more be a flood to destroy the earth...I do set my bow in the cloud, and it shall be for a token of a covenant between me and the earth" (Genesis 9: 8-13).

A CHIAPAS INDIAN LEGEND DESCRIBE THE RAINBOW AS A SYMBOL TO STOP RAIN.

"Chiapas Indians...say that the rainbow is a wall created to stop the passage of rain" (Nicholson. *Mexican and Central American Mythology*, p. 26).

1.12 THE BIBLE TELLS ABOUT A TOWER THAT WAS BUILT TO REACH HEAVEN.

"And they said, Go to, let us build us a city and a tower, whose top may reach into heaven; and let us make us a name, lest we be scattered abroad upon the face of the whole earth. And the LORD came down to see the city and the tower, which the children of men builded" (Genesis 11:4-5).

PAINTINGS AND LEGENDS OF AMERICAN INDIANS TELL ABOUT A TOWER THAT WAS BUILT TO REACH THE SKY.

"Votan, the supposed founder of the ancient and advanced Maya civilization, is said to have been a descendant of Noe, and to have assisted at the building of the Tower of Babel" (De Roo. *History of America before Columbus*, p. 300).

Many writers tell about the ancient American legends of a tower built to reach the sky (Glaser. *Indians or Jews?* pp. 11-12; Honore. *In Quest of the White God*, p. 33; Nicholson. *Mexican and Central American Myth*, p. 136).

1.13 ISRAELITES TELL ABOUT THE "CONFUSION OF TONGUES" AFTER THE TOWER WAS BUILT TO REACH HEAVEN.

"And the LORD came down to see the city and the tower, which the children of men builded. And the LORD said, Behold, the people is one, and they have all one language; and this they begin to do: and now nothing will be res-trained from them, which they have imagined to do. Go to, let us go down, and there confound their language, that they may not understand one another's speech" (Genesis 11:5-7).

ANCIENT AMERICAN LEGENDS TELL ABOUT THE "CONFUSION OF TONGUES."

"Further, the new rites and doctrine—of Catholicism— had many similarities to their own to commend them to the natives...the flood existed in recorded traditions... and Cholula pyramid embodied a Babel myth, the confusion of tongues..." (Bancroft. *History of Mexico*, Vol. 2, p. 182).

Many ancient American traditions tell about a confusion of tongues at the time when a tower was built to reach heaven (Glaser. *Indians or Jews?* pp. 11-12; Nicholson. *Mexican and Central American Mythology*, p. 136).

1.14 **AFTER THE CONFUSION OF TONGUES, PEOPLE WERE SCATTERED AROUND THE WORLD.**

"Therefore is the name of it called Babel; because the LORD did there confound the language of all the earth: and from thence did the Lord scatter them abroad upon the face of all the earth" (Genesis 11:9).

MAYAN TRADITIONS AGREE WITH THE BIBLE.

"Votan, the supposed founder of the ancient and advanced Maya civilization, is said to have been a descendant of Noe, and to have assisted at the building of the Tower of Babel. After the confusion of tongues he led a portion of the dispersed people to America, where he established the Kingdom of Chibalba and built the city of Palenque" (De Roo. *History of America before Columbus*, p. 300).

1.15 **THE BIBLE TELLS A STORY ABOUT A LADDER EXTENDING FROM HEAVEN TO EARTH.**

"And he (Jacob) dreamed, and behold a ladder set up on the earth, and the top of it reached to heaven: and behold the angels of God ascending and descending on it" (Genesis 28:12).

SOME ANCIENT AMERICANS TELL ABOUT A LADDER EXTENDING FROM HEAVEN TO EARTH.

Quetzalcoatl, the bearded white god came down from heaven to earth on a ladder. Two other gods followed him (Nicholson. *Mexican and Central American Mythology*, p. 83).

1.16 **THE "PENTATEUCH" OF THE ISRAELITES IS THE DIVINE BOOKS OF MOSES...**

The first five books in the Old Testament are attributed to Moses. They are called the Pentateuch, or the Torah.

THE TEOAMOXTLE OF ANCIENT AMERICA IS THE DIVINE BOOK OF MOSES.

"Lord Kingsborough...has discovered that the *Teoamoxtli* was the Pentateuch. Thus, *teo* means 'divine,' *amotl*, 'paper' or 'book,' and *moxtli* 'appears to be Moses,' – Divine Book of Moses" (Prescott. *History of the Conquest of Mexico*, Vol. 1, pp. 120-121).

1.17   THE ISRAELITES BELIEVED THEY WERE THE CHOSEN PEOPLE OF GOD.
"For thou art an holy people unto the Lord thy God: the Lord thy God hath chosen thee to be a special people unto himself, above all people that are upon the face of the earth" (Deuteronomy 7:6, 14:2; Joshua 24:22; 1 Kings 3:8; Isaiah 43:20).
SOME ANCIENT AMERICANS BELIEVED THEY WERE THE CHOSEN PEOPLE OF GOD.
Nahua, the name of the people in the central Mexican plateau, means "one who speaks with authority," because they were a *chosen people* who spoke for the gods (Nicholson. *Mexican and Central American Mythology*, p.15).

1.18   THE ISRAELITES BELIEVED THEY HAD THE POWER OF GOD, DIVINE AUTHORITY, TO PERFORM IN HIS NAME.
"And Moses did as the LORD commanded him: and he took Joshua, and set him before Eleazar the priest, and before all the congregation; And he laid his hands upon him, and gave him a charge, as the LORD commanded by the hand of Moses" (Numbers 27:22-23).
THE ANCIENT AMERICANS BELIEVED THEY HAD THE POWER OF GOD, DIVINE AUTHORITY, TO PERFORM IN HIS NAME.
Nahua, the name of the people in the central Mexican plateau, *means "one who speaks with authority,"* because they were a chosen people who spoke for the gods (Nicholson. *Mexican and Central American Mythology*, p.15).

1.19   THE ISRAELITE'S "POWER OF GOD" WAS CALLED THE "PRIESTHOOD."
"And thou shalt anoint them, as thou didst anoint their father, that they may minister unto me in the priest's office: for their anointing shall surely be an everlasting priesthood throughout their generations" (Exodus 40:15).
"And he shall have it, and his seed after him, even the covenant of an everlasting priesthood" (Numbers 25:13).
THE ANCIENT AMERICAN'S "POWER OF GOD" WAS CALLED THE "PRIESTHOOD."
References to "priests," "priestly order," "and "priesthood" are abundant in the writings about ancient America.

See the following:
(Burland, C.A. *The Gods of Mexico*, pp. x, 37, 57, 64, 66, 70, 78, 93, 95, 116, 131, 152, 153 and 154; Brundage. *The Fifth Sun*, pp. 114-115 and 123; Honore, Pierre. *In Quest of the White God*, p. 34; Makemson, Maud Worcester. *The Book of the Jaguar Priest, The Book of Chilam Balam of Tizimin*, p. 15; Nicholson. *Mexican and Central American Mythology*, pp. 15, 78, 79, 83, 120, 131-and132; Prescott, William H. *History of the Conquest of Mexico*, Vol. 2, p. 5;Roys. , Ralph L., *The Book of Chilam Balam of Chumayel*, p. 133;Toor, Frances. *A Treasury of Mexican Folkways*, pp. xxiv and 104)

1.20   MELCHIZEDEK WAS KNOWN AMONG THE ISRAELITES.
"And Melchizedek king of Salem was the priest of the most high God" (Genesis 14:18).
"Thou art a priest for ever after the order of Melchizedek" (Psalm 110:4).
MELCHIZEDEK WAS KNOWN AMONG THE ANCIENT AMERICANS.
"Thus it was recorded <by> the first sage, Melchize <dek>...Written *Merchise* in the Maya text. The presence of an *r* indicates a European word or name, but it does not follow that it was an *r* in Spanish. *R* and *I* sounded alike to the Mayan ear..." (Roys. *The Book of Chilam Balam of Chumayel*, p. 116).

1.21   THE OFFICE OF HIGH PRIEST WAS AMONG THE ISRAELITES.
"Go up to Hilkiah the high priest..." (2 Kings 22:4).
"Then Eliashib the high priest rose up..." (Nehemiah 3:1).
"And he shewed me Joshua the high priest standing before the angel of the LORD..." (Zechariah 3:1).
THE OFFICE OF HIGH PRIEST WAS AMONG SOME ANCIENT AMERICANS.
The high priest was next in authority to the emperor among the Aztecs. He supervised the workers of the Temples (Burland, C.A. *The Gods of Mexico*, p. 64).

1.22   ANCESTORS OF THE ISRAELITES WERE NAMED "ABRAHAM, ISAAC, AND Jacob."
"...The Lord God of your fathers, the God of Abraham, of Isaac, and of Jacob appeared unto me (Moses)..." (Exodus 3:16).
Jacob's name was changed to "Israel" (See Genesis 32:28) and his descendants became the "Israelites."
ANCESTORS OF SOME ANCIENT AMERICANS WERE NAMED "ABRAM, ESAAK, AND YACOOB."

"My guide was Indian...He told me that in very ancient time his forefathers were called Abram, Esaak, and Yacoob" (Lee, J. Fitzgerald. *The Great Migration,* p. 36; quoting an eighteenth century Dutch Jew named Aaron Levy).

1.23   JACOB WAS NAMED ISRAEL, THE ANCESTOR OF THE ISRAELITES AND HE HAD TWELVE SONS.
"...Now the sons of Jacob were twelve" (Genesis 35:22).
AN ANCESTOR OF THE AMERICAN INDIANS HAD TWELVE SONS.
"They have traditions that all Indian tribes descended from one man who had twelve sons" (Colton. *Origin of the American Indians*).

1.24   ONE OF THE ISRAELITE TWELVE SONS WAS NAMED REUBEN.
"...Now the sons of Jacob were twelve... Reuben" (Genesis 35:22-26).
ONE OF THE AMERICAN INDIAN TWELVE SONS WAS NAMED ROOBEN.
"My guide was Indian...his forefathers were called Abram, Esaak and Yakoob, that the name of his own tribe was *Rooben*" (J. Fitzgerald Lee. *The Great Migration,* p. 36; quoting an eighteenth century Dutch Jew named Aaron Levy).

1.25   THE ISRAELITES WERE DIVIDED INTO "TRIBES."
The famous "Twelve Tribes of Israel," were named after the twelve sons of Jacob, who was renamed, "Israel" (See Numbers 1:1-16 and Genesis 32:28).
THE AMERICAN INDIANS ARE DIVIDED INTO "TRIBES."
Some of the most popular American Indian "tribes" are: Alute, Apache, Aztec, Bannock, Blackfeet, Cherokee, Cheyenne, Chippewa, Cocapaw, Comanche, Eskimo, Hopi, Inca, Maya, Mohawk, Navaho, Olmec, Oneida, Pueblo, Seminole, Seneca, Shoshone, Sioux, Toltec and Ute.

1.26   TWELVE LEADERS WERE AMONG THE ISRAELITES.
"...there shall be a man of every tribe; every one head of the house of is fathers. And these are the names of the men...Elizur, Shelumiel, Nahshon , Nethaneel, Elias, Elishama, Gamaliel, Abidan, Ahiezer, Pagiel, Eliasaph, Ahira... were the—twelve—heads of thousands in Israel" (Numbers 1:4-16).
TWELVE LEADERS WERE AMONG SOME ANCIENT AMERICANS.

"...A court of (Aztec) twelve judges sat in one part of the *tianguez,* clothed with those ample and summary powers..." (Prescott. *History of the Conquest of Mexico,* Vol. 2, p. 140).

The Incas and Mayans each had twelve men who ruled them (Honore. *In Quest of the White God,* p. 66; Makemson. *The Book of the Jaguar Priest,* p. 102; Von Hagen. *The Ancient Sun Kingdoms of the Americas,* p. 354).

1.27   **THE SERPENT WAS A SACRED SYMBOL AMONG THE ISRAELITES.**

"And the LORD said unto Moses, Make thee a fiery serpent, and set it upon a pole: and it shall come to pass, that every one that is bitten, when he looketh upon it, shall live. And Moses made a serpent of brass, and put it upon a pole, and it came to pass, that if a serpent had bitten any man, when he beheld the serpent of brass, he lived" (Numbers 21:8-9).

"And the LORD said unto him (Moses),What is that in thine hand? And he said, a rod. And he said, Cast it on the ground. And he cast it on the ground, and it became a serpent...That they (the Egyptians) may believe that the LORD God...hath appeared unto thee" (Exodus 4:2-5).

THE SERPENT WAS A SACRED SYMBOL AMONG THE ANCIENT AMERICANS.

The feathered serpent was the symbol of the famous bearded white god who visited ancient America about the time of Christ. His Aztec name was Quetzalcoatl, his Mayan name was Kukulcan and his Guatemalan name was Gucumatz. All three names mean "feathered serpent" (Burland, C.A. *The Gods of Mexico,* p. 148; Nicholson. *Mexican and Central American Mythology,* 78).

(See Section Four: *Jesus Christ was in Ancient America,* the parallels of Jesus Christ and Quetzalcoatl, the Feathered Serpent God of Ancient America).

1.28   **THE HISTORY OF THE ISRAELITES INCLUDE—A SERPENT SWALLOWING OTHER SERPENTS.**

"And Moses and Aaron went in unto Pharaoh, and they did so as the Lord had commanded: and Aaron cast down his rod before Pharaoh, and before his servants, and it became a serpent. Then Pharaoh also called the wise men and the sorcerers: now the magicians of Egypt, they also did in like manner with their enchantments. For they cast down every man his rod, and they became serpents: but Aaron's rod (serpent) swallowed up their rods (serpents)" (Exodus 7:10-12).

THE HISTORY OF THE ANCIENT AMERICANS INCLUDE—A SERPENT SWALLOWING OTHER SERPENTS.

"The curious symbol of one serpent swallowing up others, likewise occurs in the nineteenth page of the *Borgian ms*" (Kingsborough. *Antiquities of Mexico,* Vol. 6, p. 401).

1.29   THE ISRAELITES TELL ABOUT WATER COMING FROM A MIRACULOUS ROCK.
"And Moses and Aaron gathered the congregation together before the rock, and he said unto them, Hear now, ye rebels; must we fetch you water out of this rock? And Moses lifted up his hand, and with his rod he smote the rock twice: and the water came out abundantly, and the congregation drank, and their beasts also" (Numbers 20:10-11).
THE ANCIENT AMERICANS TELL ABOUT WATER COMING FROM A MIRACULOUS ROCK.
"The promontory of Chapultepec, which jutted out into Lake Texcoco—just west of the island city of Tenochtitlan, Mexico— was thought to be that rock through which one gained entrance to the other world of Cincaqlso, the House of Maiaze. The water gushing out from the base of the rock had caused the original sanctity of the place..." (Brundage. *The Fifth Sun, p. 48).*

1.30   "MIRIAM" THE HEBREW WAS SHUT OUT SEVERAL DAYS FROM THE CAMP FOR COMPLAINING AGAINST HER BROTHER.
Miriam complained against her brother Moses, the Prophet of the Lord, and as a result, she was shut out from the camp for seven days (See Numbers 12:14-16).
"CHIMALMAN" THE AZTEC WAS SHUT OUT SEVERAL DAYS FROM THE CAMP FOR COMPLAINING AGAINST HER BROTHERS.
"A curious feature of identity in the Hebrew and Aztec migration is with reference to Miriam, who, under the name of Chimalman, was shut out several days from the Aztlan camp in consequence of her quarrel with her brothers, the leaders of the Aztecs or Mexicans" (Kingsborough. *Antiquities of Mexico,* Vol. 6, p. 402).

1.31   THE HISTORY OF THE HEBREWS INCLUDE TEN PLAGUES AGAINST THEIR ENEMIES.
Ten plagues came upon the Egyptians because they would not free the Israelites. Rivers turned to blood, frog invasion. lice, flies, cattle disease, boils on humans and animals, hailstorms destroyed crops, locusts, darkness, and death of the firstborn of every Egyptian home (See Exodus chapters 7-14).
THE HISTORY OF ANCIENT MEXICO INCLUDE TEN PLAGUES AGAINST THEIR ENEMIES.

"A very remarkable representation of the ten plagues which God sent on Egypt occurs in the eleventh and twelfth pages of the *Borgian ms*...These plagues were frogs, locusts, lice, flies, darkness, death of the firstborn etc." (Kingsborough. *Antiquities of Mexico,* Vol. 6, p. 401).

1.32   **THE ISRAELITES TELL OF THE PARTING OF A SEA, WITH PEOPLE WALKING THROUGH IT ON DRY GROUND.**
"And the LORD said unto Moses...lift up thou thy rod, and stretch out thine hand over the sea, and divide it: and the children of Israel shall go on dry ground through the midst of the sea...And Moses stretched out his hand over the sea; and the LORD caused the sea to go back by a strong east wind all that night, and made the sea dry land, and the waters were divided. And the children of Israel went into the midst of the sea upon the dry ground; and the waters were a wall unto them on their right hand, and on their left" (Exodus 14:15-22).
THE ANCIENT AMERICANS TELL OF THE PARTING OF A SEA, WITH PEOPLE WALKING THROUGH IT ON DRY GROUND.
"The people of Yucatan have a tradition that they came originally from the Far East, passing through the sea, which God made dry for them..." (Bancroft. *The Native Races of the Pacific States,* Vol. 5, p. 22). The story is told that the heroes of the migration had a staff which they used to separate the sea and cause the ground to appear so they could cross over to the distant shore (Nicholson. *Mexican and Central American Mythology, p.* 135).
"It is not quite clear, however, how they crossed the sea; they crossed to this side, as if there were no sea...they crossed the sea, the waters having parted when they passed" (Goetz and Morley. *Popol Vuh,* p. 183).

1.33   **AFTER THE ISRAELITES WALKED THROUGH THE PARTING SEA, THE WATER RETURNED AND KILLED THEIR PURSUERS.**
"And Moses stretched forth his hand over the sea, and the sea returned to his strength when the morning appeared, and the Egyptians fled against it; and the Lord overthrew the Egyptians in the midst of the sea. And the waters returned, and covered the chariots, and the horsemen, and all the host of Pharaoh that came into the sea after them, there remained not so much as one of them" (Exodus 14:27-28).
AFTER THE ANCIENT AMERICANS WALKED THROUGH THE PARTING SEA, THE WATER RETURNED AND KILLED THEIR PURSUERS.

"Other stories tell of Quetzalcoatl walking across the sea, or even marching through it, when the sea would fall and engulf his pursuers" (Burland, C.A. *The Gods of Mexico,* p. 161).

1.34 **THE ISRAELITES HAD AN "ARK OF THE COVENANT," A HOLY CHEST THEY CARRIED INTO BATTLE.**
The Ark of the Covenant was a holy chest made out of wood and laid with gold. It contained some holy objects pertaining to the history of the Hebrews, such as the tablets of the Ten Commandments and a pot of manna.
This Ark of the Covenant was carried on men's shoulders into battle (See Exodus 25:10-22; 1 Samuel 4:4-7 and 1 Chronicles 15:15).
THE ANCIENT AMERICAN INDIANS HAD AN "ARK OF THE COVENANT," A HOLY CHEST THEY CARRIED INTO BATTLE.
"On the excellent authority of Adair, Long, and Noah, American historians and ethnologists, we are informed that the western tribes of the North American Indians kept a holy chest, or ark, which they were wont to carry to the battlefield when hard pressed by their enemies. Long says: 'This ark was placed on a sort of frame carried on men's shoulders, and was not allowed to touch the ground'" (Lee, J. Fitzgerald. *The Great Migration,* p. 109).

1.35 **IT WAS FORBIDDEN FOR THE ORDINARY PERSON TO TOUCH THE ISRAELITE ARK OF THE COVENANT.**
"And when they came to Nachon's threshing floor, Uzzah put forth his hand to the ark of God, and took hold of it; for the oxen shook it. And the anger of the Lord was kindled against Uzzah; and God smote him there for his error; and there he died by the ark of God" (2 Samuel 6:6-7).
IT WAS FORBIDDEN FOR THE ORDINARY PERSON TO TOUCH THE ANCIENT AMERICAN ARK OF THE COVENANT.
"This ark was placed on a sort of frame carried on men's shoulders, and was not allowed to touch the ground. To uncover it was strictly forbidden. Three men who out of curiosity attempted to examine its contents were struck blind on the spot" (Lee, J. Fitzgerald. *The Great Migration, p.* 109).

1.36 **THE HONEYBEE WAS VERY PROMINENT IN THE LAND OF THE HEBREWS.**
"And I am come down to deliver them out of the hand of the Egyptians, and to bring them up out of that land unto a good land and a large, unto a land flowing with milk and honey..." (Exodus 3:8).
The word "honey" is found fifty-two times in the Old Testament.

"And John was clothed with camel's hair and with a girdle of a skin about his loins: and he did eat locusts and wild honey" (Mark 1:6).

THE HONEYBEE WAS VERY PROMINENT IN ANCIENT AMERICA.

Bees and honey in ancient America is mentioned many times in many books. Some books say the bees were stingless.

(Makemson. *The Book of the Jaguar Priest,* translation of *The book of Chilam Balam of Tizimin,* pp. 6, 139, 141,144; Toor. *A Treasury of Mexican Folkways,* p. 24; Von Hagen. *The Ancient Sun Kingdoms of the Americas,* pp. 208-209, 239; Roys. *The Book of Chilam Balam of Chumayel,* p. 63-65, see also pp. 9, 95, 97, 101,104, 117, 131,171, and 190)

This should settle the false theory of some writers who have said that file honey bee was introduced into America by the Spanish.

1.37   **THE ISRAELITES PROPHESIED THAT THEY WOULD BE SCATTERED OVER THE EARTH.**

"And thy (Jacob's) seed shall be as the dust of the earth, and thou shalt spread abroad to the west, and to the east, and to the north, and to the south; and in thee and in thy seed shall all the families of the earth be blessed" (Genesis 28:14).

"And they shall know that I am the LORD, when I shall scatter them among the nations, and disperse them in the countries" (Ezekiel 12:15).

ANCIENT AMERICAN TRADITIONS SAY THAT THE FIRST SETTLERS CAME FROM THE EAST BY WATER, OVER THE ATLANTIC OCEAN.

"Landa says in his book that some old men of Yucatan related to him the story, handed down for many generations that the first settlers had come from the east by water (Willard. *The City of the Sacred Well,* p. 34).

"These voyagers (from the east) were ones 'whom God had freed, opening for them twelve roads to the sea.' If there is any truth in this tradition, these progenitors may have been one of the lost tribes of Israel" (Willard. *The City of the Sacred Well,* p. 35).

1.38   **THE ISRAELITES BELIEVED THAT THEY WERE GIVEN A PROMISED LAND.**

"And it shall come to pass, when ye be come to the land which the LORD will give you, according as he hath promised, that he shall keep this service" (Exodus 12:25).

"And thou shalt write unto them all the words of this law, when thou art passed over, that thou mayest go in unto the land which the LORD thy God giveth thee, a land that floweth with milk and honey;

as the LORD God of thy fathers hath promised thee" (Deuteronomy 27:3).

THE ANCIENT AMERICANS BELIEVED THAT THEY WERE GIVEN A PROMISED LAND.

"When the priests and elders saw the place, they wept for joy and said: 'Now we have reached the promised land, now we have seen what comfort and rest has been bestowed upon the Mexican people. Nothing more remains for us. O be comforted, sons and brothers, for we have now discovered and achieved what our God promised you...'" (Nicholson. *Mexican and Central American Mythology*, p. 131-132).

1.39   THE HEBREW LANGUAGE IS VERY SIMILAR TO THE AMERICAN INDIAN LANGUAGE.

Hebrew or Chaldaic	American-Indian	English
Ale, Aleim	Ale	God
Shiloh	Shilu	Shiloh
Abba	Abba	Father
Ish	Ish, Ishte	Man
Ishto	Ishto	Woman
Eweh, Eve	Awah	Wife
Lihene	Liani	His Wife
Neheri	Nieniri	Nose
Korah	Kora	Winter
Phalac	Phale	To pray

(See Smith, *View of the Hebrews, or the Tribes of Israel in America*, 1825 Edition, p. 90)

These are only ten of the thirty-three comparisons listed in his book. Smith, the author, says: "Some of these Indian words are taken from one tribe, and some from another" (p. 90).

1.40   HEBREW ART.

Ancient Hebrew sculptures and murals are found all over modern Israel. How do they compare with those found in the ancient America cities?

ANCIENT AMERICAN ART.

"... the first settlers had come from the east by water. These voyagers were ones 'whom God had freed, opening for them twelve roads to the sea.' If there is any truth in this tradition, these progenitors may have been one of the lost tribes of Israel. An interesting side light on this hypothesis is the distinctly Semitic cast of countenance of some of the ancient sculptures and murals found at Chichen Itza and in other old Maya cities. The dignity of face and serene poise of these carved or painted likenesses is strikingly Hebraic" (Willard. *The City of the Sacred Well*, pp 35-36).

1.41 JUDAIC EVIDENCES IN ANCIENT AMERICA?

Judaism is a part of the Hebrew culture. Not all Hebrew are Jews in history, but all Jews are Hebrews, either by ancestral descent or by adoption through conversion.

JUDAIC EVIDENCES IN ANCIENT AMERICA!

"Spaniards discerned in the...Aztec religion the features...of the Jewish and Christian revelations" (Prescott. *Conquest of Mexico*, Vol. 2, p. 154).

Chapter Two of *Indians or Jews* is entitled, The Ten Tribes of Israel (Glaser. *Indians or Jews?* pp. 3-8).

Evidences discovered in America show that many things were originated by the Jews (Nicholson. *Mexican and Central American Mythology, p.* 19; Von Hagen. The *Ancient Sun Kingdoms of the Americas,* p. 19; 41, and 42; Willard. *The City of the Sacred Well*, p.36, footnotes).

1.42 A SABBATICAL COUNT OF SEVEN DAYS WAS COMMON AMONG THE ISRAELITES.

"Remember the *sabbath* day, to keep it holy. Six days shalt thou labour, and do all thy work: But the seventh day is the sabbath of the LORD thy God: in it thou shalt not do any work, thou, nor thy son, nor thy daughter, thy man-servant, nor thy maidservant, nor thy cattle, nor thy stranger that is within thy gates: For in six days the LORD made heaven and earth, the sea, and all that in them is, and rested the seventh day: wherefore the LORD blessed the sabbath day, and hallowed it" (Exodus 20:8-11).

A SABBATICAL COUNT OF SEVEN DAYS WAS COMMON AMONG THE ANCIENT AMERICANS:

The number seven was very important to the American Indians: the number one is *east*, two is *south*, three is *west*, four is *north*, five is *top*, six is *bottom* and seven is *center* which signifies universality.

Lord Kingsborough suggested that the sabbatical count was introduced to the ancient Mexicans by Jewish theologians (Burland, C.A. *The Gods of Mexico*, p. 83).

1.43 A DAY FOR THE JEWS STARTED AND ENDED AT SUNSET.

"For the Jews, the day always belonged to the previous night...The day lasted till three stars became visible...In regard to the Passover, it is distinctly stated that it began with the darkness on the 14th Nisan" (Ebersheim. *The Life and Times of Jesus the Messiah*, Vol.2, pp. 468-469).

A DAY FOR THE AZTECS STARTED AND ENDED AT SUNSET.

"The Aztec day ran from sunset to sunset, and the contrast of night and day formed the basis of astrological reckoning" (Burland and Forman. *The Aztecs,* p. 101).

1.44 TEMPLE WORSHIP WAS IMPORTANT TO THE ISRAELITES.

"... Thus saith the LORD, Shalt thou build me an house for me to dwell in?" (2 Samuel 7:5).

"But the LORD is in his holy temple: let all the earth keep silence before him" (Habakkuk 2:20).

TEMPLE WORSHIP WAS IMPORTANT TO MANY ANCIENT AMERICANS.

The most sacred places in ancient America were the many temples which were located among various tribes like the Great Temple of Quetzalcoatl at Teotihuacán, the Temple of Kukulkaan at Chichen Itza, and the one at Tenochtitlan to name a few (Carrasco. *Religions of Mesoamerica,* p. 70; Toor. *A Treasury of Mexican Folkways,* p. 104).

1.45 THE TEMPLES OF THE ISRAELITES WERE NOT OPEN TO THE PUBLIC, ONLY TO THE CHOSEN PEOPLE OF GOD.

"Thus was the first enclosure (of the temple). In the midst of which, and not far from it, was the second, to be gone up to by a few steps: this was encompassed by a stone wall for a partition, with an inscription, which forbade any foreigner to go in under pain of death" (*Josephus Complete Works,* p. 336).

THE TEMPLES OF THE TOLTEC INDIANS WERE NOT OPEN TO THE PUBLIC, ONLY TO THE CHOSEN PEOPLE OF GOD.

"...there is the temple of the knot of Xipe, only open to those of Toltec descent" (Nicholson. *Mexican and Central American Mythology,* p. 83).

Only noblemen who were believers of Quetzalcoatl could enter the Temple (Burland, C.A. *The Gods of Mexico, p.* 148).

1.46 THE TEMPLES OF THE HEBREWS HAD A ROOM CALLED THE "MOST HOLY PLACE" OR THE "HOLY OF HOLIES."

"The Most Holy Place, or Holy of Holies... West fifteen feet of the Tabernacle, a perfect cube, represented God's Dwelling Place. It contained only the ark. It was entered by the High priest once a year. A *shadow of heaven*" (*Halley's Bible Handbook,* p. 130).

"And thou shalt put the mercy seat upon the ark of the testimony in the most holy place" (Exodus 26:34).

"In the most holy place shalt thou eat it; every male shall eat it shall be holy unto thee" (Numbers 18:10).

THE TEMPLES OF THE ANCIENT AMERICANS HAD A ROOM CALLED THE "MOST HOLY PLACE" OR THE "HOLY OF HOLIES."

The temple was dedicated to Viracocha, another name for Quetzalcoatl, and in the temple was the "Sanctisimum," the Holy of Holies (Honore. *In Quest of the White God,* pp. 148-149).

On top of the *Castillo de Kukulcan* at Chichen Itza in the Yucatan, there is a small temple with two rooms. The front room has a column of stone with a carving of the bearded god Kukulcan—the Maya name for Quetzalcoatl—and it is called *el cuarto sagrado,* the holy room. Behind the holy room there is a smaller room in the center of the temple which is called *el cuarto mas sagrado,* the most holy room (Per the author's tour in February 1981).

1.47   **ISRAELITE PRIESTS HAD HOLY GARMENTS.**

"And thou shalt make holy garments for Aaron thy brother for glory and for beauty" (Exodus 28:2).

QUETZALCOATL PRIESTS HAD HOLY GARMENTS.

"At that time his loin-cloth and his mantle shall be white, a reference to the white garments of the priests of Quetzalcoatl" (Roys. *The Book of Chilam Balam of Chumayel,* p. 133).

The priests had a sacred symbol on their garments. It was a white cross in a black background (Burland, C.A. *The Gods of Mexico,* p. 131).

1.48   **THE ISRAELITES RECORDED A TIME WHEN THE SUN STOOD STILL.**

"Then spake Joshua to the LORD in the day when the LORD delivered up the Amorites before the children of Israel, and he said in the sight of Israel, Sun, stand thou still upon Gideon; and thou, Moon, in the valley of Ajalon. And the sun stood still, and the moon stayed, until the people had avenged themselves upon their enemies" (Joshua 10:12-13).

THE ANCIENT AMERICANS RECORDED A TIME WHEN THE SUN STOOD STILL.

The sun stood still when the symbolism of the plumed serpent was developed (Nicholson. *Mexican and Central American Mythology,* p. 12).

1.49   **HISTORY REPEATS ITSELF, ACCORDING TO THE ISRAELITES.**

"The thing that hath been, it is that which shall be; and thin which is done is that which shall be done: and there is no new thing under the sun. Is there any thing whereof it may be said, See, this is new? It hath been already of old time, which was before us" (Ecclesiastes 1:9-10).

HISTORY REPEATS ITSELF, ACCORDING TO THE ANCIENT AMERICANS.

"The Maya believed that history tends to repeat itself in regular cycles. They drew their prophecies of future events from the abundant records of the past; and when they chronicled historical data on monuments of stone or in books of bark paper, it was with full recognition of their importance in determining the 'shape of things to come'" (Makemson. *The Book of the Jaguar Priest* translation of *The book of Chilam Balam of Tizimin,* p. 97 and 106).

1.50   **THE BIBLE STORY OF "DAVID AND BATHSHEBA" IS VERY SIMILAR TO A STORY TOLD BY SOME ANCIENT AMERICANS.**

"...David arose from off his bed, and walked upon the roof of the king's house: and from the roof he saw a woman washing herself; and the woman was very beautiful to look upon. And David sent and enquired after the woman...And one said, Is not this Bathsheba...the wife of Uriah the Hittite? And David sent messengers, and took her; and she came in unto him, and he lay with her...And the woman conceived, and sent and told David, and said, I am with child...And he wrote in the letter, saying, Set ye Uriah in the forefront of the hottest battle, and retire ye from him, that he may be smitten, and die...and Uriah the Hittite died..." (2 Samuel 11:2-17).

THE   ANCIENT   AMERICAN   STORY   OF "NEZAHUALCOYOTL AND HEBE."

King Nezahualcoyotl, "...was captivated by the grace and personal charms of the youthful Hebe, and conceived a violent passion for her...He accordingly sent an order to the chief of Tepechpan—the husband of Hebe—to take command of an expedition set on foot against the Tlascalans. At the same time he instructed two Tezcucan chiefs to keep near the person of the old lord, and bring him into the thickest of the fight, where he might lose his life...His predictions were soon verified...and he expressed his deep sympathy for her loss...When his courtiers had acquainted him with her name and rank, he ordered her to be conducted to the palace, that she might receive the attentions due to her station. The interview was soon followed by a public declaration of his passion; and the marriage was celebrated not long after...This story, which furnishes so obvious a counterpart to that of David and Uriah, is told with great circumstantiality..." (Prescott. *History of the Conquest of Mexico,* Vol. 1, pp. 189-190).

1.51   MULTIPLE WIVES AND CONCUBINES (POLYGAMY) WAS COMMON AMONG THE ISRAELITES.
Abram's wives: Sarai and Hagar (See Genesis 16:1-3).
Abraham had sons from concubines (See Genesis 25:6).
Jacob had 12 sons with four wives (See Genesis 29-30).
There were laws pertaining to multiple wives (See Exodus 21:10-11).
"If a man have two wives..." (Deuteronomy 21:15).
David had concubines and wives (See 2 Samuel 5:13).
The LORD gave David his wives (See 2 Samuel 12:7-8).
Caleb, the righteous, had three wives and three concubines (See 1 Chronicles 2:18-19).
Abijah, had 14 wives (See 2 Chronicles 13:21).
Joash "...did that which was right in the sight of the Lord...." He had two wives (See 2 Chronicles 24:2-3).
MULTIPLE WIVES AND CONCUBINES (POLYGAMY) WAS COMMON AMONG THE ANCIENT AMERICANS.
"Concubinage existed in Aztec life" (Von Hagen. *The Ancient Sun Kingdoms of the Americas,* p. 73, see also p. 495). The Emperor Moctezuma had a thousand wives and concubines (Leornard. *Ancient America,* p. 143).

1.52   ISRAELITE KING SOLOMON HAD 1,000 WIVES AND CONCUBINAGES.
"But king Solomon loved many strange women...And he had seven hundred wives, princesses, and three hundred concubines: and his wives turned away his heart" (1 Kings 11:1-3).
AMERICAN EMPEROR MOCTEZUMA HAD 1,000 WIVES AND CONCUBINAGES.
"The Emperor came to call on the Spaniard and invited him to his own palace, where he lived in vast magnificence with hordes of courtiers and a thousand wives and concubines" (Leonard. *Ancient America,* p. 143).

1.53   ADULTERY WAS PUNISHED BY DEATH AMONG THE ISRAELITES.
"And the man that committeth adultery with another man's wife, even he that committeth adultery with his neighbour's wife, the adulterer and the adulteress shall surely be put to death" (Leviticus 20:10).
ADULTERY WAS PUNISHED BY DEATH AMONG THE ANCIENT AMERICANS.
"The laws of the Aztecs were registered, and exhibited to the people in their hieroglyphical paintings...Adulterers, as among the Jews, were stoned to death" (Prescott. *History of the Conquest of Mexico,* Vol. 1, p. 59).

Writers have recorded that Ancient Americans taught their people to avoid adultery or they would be punished harshly (Burland C.A. *The Gods of Mexico*, p. 101; Von Hagen. *The Ancient Sun Kingdoms of the Americas*, pp. 72 and 480).

1.54 CIRCUMCISION WAS PRACTICED AMONG THE ISRAELITE.

"And God said unto Abraham...This is my covenant, which ye shall keep, between me and you and thy seed after thee; Every man child among you shall be circumcised. And ye shall circumcise the flesh of your foreskin; and it shall be a token of the covenant betwixt me and you" (Genesis 17:9-11).

CIRCUMCISION WAS PRACTICED AMONG THE ANCIENT AMERICANS.

"The American Indians have practiced circumcision...circumcision was long ago practiced among them, but that their young men made a mock of it, and it fell into disrepute and was discontinued" (Smith. *View of the Hebrews, or the Tribes of Israel in America*, 1825 Edition, p. 90).

Ancient Maya and Peruvian boys were circumcised (Honore. *In Quest of the White God*, p. 35; Von Hagen. *The Ancient Sun Kingdoms of the Americas*, p. 42).

1.55 THE ISRAELITES BELIEVED THAT THERE MUST BE OPPOSITION IN ALL THINGS.

"To every thing there is a season, and a time to every purpose under the heaven; A time to be born, and a time to die; a time to plant, and a time to pluck up that which is planted; A time to kill, and a time to heal; a time to break down, and a time to build up; A time to weep, and a time to laugh; a time to mourn, and a time to dance; a time to cast away stones, and a time to gather stones together; a time to embrace, and a time to refrain from embracing; a time to get, and a time to lose; a time to keep, and a time to cast away; a time to rend, and a time to sew; a time to keep silence, and a time to speak; a time to love, and a time to hate; a time of war, and a time of peace" (Ecclesiastes 3:1-10).

THE ANCIENT AMERICANS BELIEVED THAT THERE MUST BE OPPOSITION IN ALL THINGS.

Opposing factors, such as male and female, light and dark, movement and stillness, order and disorder were essential. It was opposition that life came into being (Burland, C.A. *The Gods of Mexico*, p. 130).

Many people in ancient America believed opposites such as life to death, light to darkness, infinity to finitude, good to evil, spirit to matter etc. (Nicholson. *Mexican and Central American Mythology*, pp. 23, 89 and 110; Brundage. *The Fifth Sun*, p. 126).

1.56 THERE WAS MEDITERRANEAN LEARNING IN ISRAELITE HISTORY.

Father Abraham lived in Egypt, on the shore of the Mediterranean Sea, for an unspecified time (Genesis 12:10-14). Joseph was sold into Egypt and later brought all of his family, the children of Israel, to live in Egypt with him (Genesis 37:28; 50:22).

The children of Israel remained in Egypt for at least four hundred years (Genesis 15:13 and Exodus 12:40), during this time they obviously adopted much of the Egyptian culture, and other cultures on the Mediterranean. Also, their own "Promised Land" was located on the eastern end of the Mediterranean Sea.

THERE ARE MEDITERRANEAN WRITINGS FOUND IN ANCIENT AMERICAN HISTORY.

There is evidence that the New England area of the United States and also South American countries were visited by Mediterranean people. Celtic, Basque, Phoenician and Egyptian writings have been found there (Fell. *America B.C.*, pp. 282 and 291; Honore. *In Quest of the White* God, p. 141; Von Hagen. *The Ancient Sun Kingdoms of the Americas*, p. 19).

1.57 IS EGYPTIAN CULTURE AND ART FOUND IN ANCIENT AMERICAN HISTORY?

After living four hundred years in Egypt, the children of Israel most likely learned the Egyptian culture and art.

YES—EGYPTIAN CULTURE AND ART ARE FOUND IN ANCIENT AMERICAN HISTORY.

"It (the temple) stood in the midst of a vast area...ornamented on the outer side by figures of serpents, raised in relief, which gave it the name of the *atepantli*, or *wall of serpents*. This emblem was a common one in the sacred sculpture of 'Anahuac Mexico, as well as of Egypt" (Prescott. *History of the Conquest of Mexico*, Vol. 2, p. 142, see also p. 153).

For more Egyptian culture and art in New Mexico and Central America, see: Fell, *America B.C.*, pp. 175; 190 and 191; Honore. *In Quest of the White God*, pp.115 and p. 142 and; Nicholson, *Mexican and Central American Mythology, p.* 16.

1.58 ISRAELITES HELPED THE EGYPTIANS BUILD PYRAMIDS.

The Israelites lived in Egypt, close to the famous pyramids for four hundred years (See Genesis 15:13; Exodus 12:40).

In fact, the Egyptians, "set them to build pyramids" (*Josephus Complete Works*, Chapter IX, p. 55).

ANCIENT AMERICANS BUILT PYRAMIDS.

Pyramids are found in only two places in the world, in Egypt and in America, specifically in Mexico, Guatemala, Honduras, and Peru (*Funk and Wagnalls New Encyclopedia*, Vol. 20, p.18).

Some of the pyramids of ancient America were built very similarly to those of the Egyptians (Honore. *In Quest of the White God*, pp.70, 91 and 154).

1.59   ARE EGYPTIAN CARVINGS SIMILAR TO THE ANCIENT AMERICAN CARVINGS?

Human figures, when Egyptians carved them on panels, walls, plates and etc, always show their heads and legs and feet in profile (side view); but the body (trunk) is always shown in front view (Newsweek Books, *Milestones of History, Ancient Empires*, p. 15).

YES —ANCIENT AMERICAN CARVINGS ARE SIMILAR TO THE EGYPTIAN CARVINGS.

"The architecture and art point to a very early stage in Mayan civilization...Heads are always shown in profile, body and arms frontally, legs and feet again in side view, with the toes of the left foot touching the heel of the right. Human figures in the ancient Egyptian relics are shown in exactly the same attitude" (Honore. *In Quest of the White God*, p. 89).

1.60   THE EGYPTIANS USED HIEROGLYPHICS.

After living in Egypt for 400 years, could it be that the Israelites brought Egyptian hieroglyphics to America?

SOME ANCIENT AMERICANS USED HIEROGLYPHICS.

"Hieroglyphics, characters in a system of writing that consist of representations of objects rather than purely conventional signs. The term is also applied to the system of writing using such characters, and especially to the writing of the Maya (q.v), early Indians of Mexico, and of the ancient Egyptians" (*Funk and Wagnalls New Encyclopedia*, Vol. 12, p. 365).

Chapter seventeen of one of the best books about ancient America is totally dedicated to the evidence that ancient Egyptians hieroglyphics existed with the people who lived in America in ancient times (Fell. *America B.C.*, pp. 253-276).

"The Indians of the golden land write in books, he said in his letters to other humanists as he analyzed the technique of the book and the hieroglyphics... 'which almost resemble those of the Egyptians...'" (The Italian humanist Pietro Martire D'Anghiere is quoted by Von Hagen, *The Ancient Sun Kingdoms of the Americas*, p. 14; see also pp. 187 and 256).

1.61 EGYPTIANS AND ANCIENT AMERICANS BUILT SIMILAR TOMBS.

"Other parallels with the Old World in architecture and building techniques include the audience chambers, rooms let into the ground; the little round hole in the top slabs of graves—exactly as on Egyptian tombs" (Honore. *In Quest of the White God*, p. 155).

1.62 EGYPTIANS PRACTICED "MUMMIFICATION."

The Hebrews lived in Egypt for four hundred years (Genesis 15:13; Exodus 12:40; Acts 7:6-7). While they were there, they must have learned much about mummification. If indeed, some Israelites came to America, that could explain why mummification existed in ancient America.

SOME ANCIENT AMERICANS PRACTICED "MUMMIFICATION."

"Mummies were known not only to the Incas and in Peru but also in Colombia...the methods of mummification were almost exactly the same as in ancient Egypt" (Honore. *In Quest of the White God*, p. 139). Embalming and mummification in Egypt and Peru were nearly identical. The Egyptians removed the internal body organs and put them in jars, cleaned the cavity with spices and wrapped the body with strips of cloth, and so did the Incas (Von Hagen. *The Ancient Sun Kingdoms of the Americas,* p. 501).

1.63 EGYPTIANS BUILT PAPYRUS BOATS, MADE OUT OF WATER REEDS.

"The *balsas* also, the boats plying on Lake Titicaca, may very well go back to the Old World. Both in construction and in material, they are amazingly like the Egyptian papyrus boats we know from reliefs" (Honore. *In Quest of the White God, p.* 155).

SOME ANCIENT AMERICANS BUILT PAPYRUS BOATS, MADE OUT OF WATER REEDS.

There are only two places in the world where boats were made out of water reeds: Egypt and Lake Titicaca in Peru. Anyone who has read the book *Ra II* by Thor Heyerdahl will know about his reed boat and his attempt to cross the Atlantic Ocean..

1.64 EGYPTIAN METALLURGY TECHNIQUES ARE FOUND IN ANCIENT AMERICA.

The metallurgy techniques in ancient Egypt were very unique. One of those techniques is found in Peru.

ANCIENT INCA METALLURGY TECHNIQUES WERE SIMILAR TO THOSE OF ANCIENT EGYPT.

After describing many of the Inca metallurgists' techniques von Hagen explains: "This technique is no different from that depicted on an Egyptian tomb at Saqqara, dating back to 2400 B.C." (Von Hagen. *The Ancient Sun Kingdoms of the Americas,* p. 531).

1.65 ANCIENT EGYPTIANS HAD ELEPHANTS.
Even though wild elephants are not found in Northern Africa near Egypt, domestic elephants have been used in Egypt for hundreds of years B.C.

"In ancient times elephants were used in war. A Greek tablet at Adulis on the Red Sea relates that about 243 B.C. an Egyptian ruler conquered considerable territory in Asia Minor with the aid of elephants captured in Abyssinia, now Ethiopia" (*Funk and Wagnalls New Encyclopedia,* 8:459).

ANCIENT AMERICANS HAD ELEPHANTS.
"One of the most intriguing things is the constant recurrence of the mask of Kukul Can, often conventionalized to fit the particular wall of a building, frieze, or mural...And always it is shown with a long upturned snout which some casual observer has called an elephant's trunk. To go a bit afield, G. Elliot Smith's *Elephants and Ethnologists* takes up this subject of the elephant's head. He believes that several elaborately carved columns or stelae in Copan, another Mayan city, possibly more ancient than Chichen Itza, present credible pictures of elephant's heads with the keepers or mahouts beside them. These carvings have caused considerable discussion; some stoutly maintain that they portray the elephant..." (Willard. *The City of the Sacred Well,* pp. 213-214).

When I, the author of this study, visited Chichen Itza in 1981, our guide told us that just a few miles south of Chichen Itza there were some carvings of elephants. Unfortunately, we did not take the time to go and see them.

1.66 PALESTINE'S NEIGHBOR IRAQ HAS A VERY SIMILAR PARALLEL IN ANCIENT AMERICA.
Iraq:
Iraq is contained within the boundaries where the old Assyrian Empire was located when the ten northern tribes of Israel were taken captive by them.
ANCIENT AMERICANS.
Basket making in Iraq are almost identical with those found in the Americas (Von Hagen, *The Ancient Sun Kingdoms of the Americas,* p.261).

1.67   A VERY UNUSUAL PERSIAN CUSTOM WAS PRACTICED IN ANCIENT AMERICA.
PERSIANS:
The Persian Empire conquered Babylon in 538 B.C. Its conquest extended into Egypt, and it held control of Judea from 530 to 334 B.C. A very unusual custom in Persia was the placing of a "burden stone" at high places at the side of major roads.
ANCIENT CHILEANS:
"On the high places along the road, the Incas, following ancient customs, placed *apachetas (apa,* 'burden,' *cheta,* 'depositor') travelers…they placed a stone on the *apacheta* as a symbol of the burden…the Persians did the same along their roads" (Von Hagen. *The Ancient Sun Kingdoms of the Americas,* pp. 544-545).

1.68   PERSIAN ROADS HAD POST HOUSES ABOUT EIGHTEEN MILES APART FOR THE ACCOMMODATION OF TRAVELERS.
The Persian Empire conquered Babylon in 538 B.C. Its conquest extended into Egypt, and it held control of Judea from 530 to 334 B.C. Persians built post houses about eighteen miles apart (Von Hagen, The *Ancient Sun Kingdoms of the Americas,* p. 550).
INCA ROADS HAD POST HOUSES ABOUT 18 MILES APART FOR THE ACCOMMODATION OF TRAVELERS.
The Inca Empire built post-houses at every four to six leagues (twelve to eighteen miles) (Von Hagen. The *Ancient Sun Kingdoms of the Americas,* p. 551).

1.69   WALLED CITIES WERE VERY COMMON IN HOLY LAND OF THE ISRAELITES.
Many near-eastern cities were surrounded by walls, such as Jerusalem (Jeremiah 52:14), Babylon (Jeremiah 51:58), Jericho (Hebrews 11:30) and Tyrus (Ezekiel 26:4).
WALLED CITIES WERE VERY COMMON IN ANCIENT AMERICA.
In Yucatan there were many walled cities of the ancient Maya. Some of their walls were fifteen feet high, completely surrounding their large towns (Von Hagen. *The Ancient Sun Kingdoms of the Americas,* p. 168, see also p. 219).

1.70   ISRAELITES BELIEVED IN THE RESURRECTION OF THE DEAD.
"Thy dead men shall live, together with my dead body shall they arise. Awake and sing, ye that dwell in dust: for thy dew is as the dew of herbs, and the earth shall cast out the dead" (Isaiah 26:19).

"Therefore prophesy and say unto them, Thus saith the LORD God; Behold, O my people, I will open your graves, and cause you to come up out of your graves, and bring you into the land of Israel" (Ezekiel 37:12).

SOME MAYA INDIANS BELIEVED IN THE RESURRECTION OF THE DEAD.

"There were a number of parallels between Maya and Christian thought, including the symbolism of the cross and the idea of death and resurrection" (Nicholson. *Mexican and Central American Mythology,* p. 21).

1.71 BETWEEN DEATH AND RESURRECTION MAN GOES TO A SPIRIT WORLD, ACCORDING TO THE ISRAELITES.

"Then Abraham gave up the ghost, and died in a good old age, an old man, and full of years; and was gathered to his people" (Genesis 25:8).

"Then shall the dust return to the earth as it was: and the spirit shall return unto God who gave it" (Ecclesiastes 12:7).

BETWEEN DEATH AND RESURRECTION MAN GOES TO A SPIRIT WORLD, ACCORDING TO MANY ANCIENT AMERICANS.

"Therefore, the ancients said that when they died, men did not perish, but began to live again almost as if awakened from a dream and that they became spirits or gods" (Carrasco. *Religions of Mesoamerica,* p. 69).

Many Ancient Americans believed that a person's spirit continues to live after death and that it passes from one phase of life to another (Nicholson. *Mexican and Central American Mythology,* p. 42; Toor. *A treasury of Mexican Folkways,* p. 160; Von Hagen. *The Ancient Sun Kingdoms of the Americas.* pp. 116. 295 and 490).

1.72 THE ISRAELITES BELIEVED IN HEAVEN

"The LORD is in his holy temple, the LORD's throne is in heaven: his eyes behold, his eyelids try, the children of men" (Psalm 11:4).

"How art thou fallen from heaven, O Lucifer, son of the morning! How art thou cut down to the ground which didst weaken the nations!" (Isaiah 14:12).

"But there is a God in heaven that revealeth secrets..." (Daniel 2:28).

SOME ANCIENT AMERICANS BELIEVED IN HEAVEN.

Some writers say the Aztecs believed that Quetzalcoatl came from heaven (Carrasco. *Religions of Mesoamerica,* pp. 44-45; Brundage. *The Fifth Sun,* p. 78).

Other writers have said that the Maya believed in heaven (Honore. *In Quest of the White* God, p. 35; Von Hagen. *The Ancient Sun Kingdoms of the Americas,* p. 295).

1.73   THE ISRAELITES BELIEVED IN HELL,
"The wicked shall be turned into hell, and all the nations that forget God" (Psalms 9:17).
"Yet thou (Babylon) shalt be brought down to hell, to the sides of the pit" (Isaiah 14:15).
ANCIENT MAYANS BELIEVED IN HELL.
"The Mayas believed in immortality and a form of heaven and hell" (Von Hagen. *The Ancient Sun Kingdoms of the Americas,* p. 295, see also p. 116).

1.74   MARRIAGE CEREMONIES WERE CONDUCTED BY ISRAELITES.
"Therefore shall a man leave his father and his mother, and shall cleave unto his wife: and they shall be one flesh" (Genesis 2:24).
MARRIAGE CEREMONIES WERE CONDUCTED BY ANCIENT AMERICANS.
"The rites of marriage were celebrated with as much formality as in any Christian country" (Prescott. *History of the Conquest of Mexico,* Vol. 1, p. 60).

1.75   DIVORCE WAS ALLOWED BY THE ISRAELITES.
"When a man hath taken a wife, and married her, and it come to pass that she find no favour in his eyes, because he hath found some uncleanness in her: then let him write her a bill of divorcement, and give it in her hand, and send her out of his house" (Deuteronomy 24:1).
DIVORCE WAS ALLOWED BY THE ANCIENT AMERICANS.
"Divorces could not be obtained, until authorized by a sentence of this court, after a patient hearing of the parties" (Prescott. *History of the Conquest of Mexico,* Vol. 1, p. 61).

1.76   ADULTERY WAS VERY EVIL AMONG THE ISRAELITES.
"Thou shalt not commit adultery" (Exodus 20:14).
"... thou shalt not covet thy neighbour's wife..." (Exodus 20:17).
ADULTERY WAS VERY EVIL AMONG THE AZTEC INDIANS.
"The laws of the Aztecs were registered, and exhibited to the people in their hieroglyphical paintings...Adulterers, as among the Jews, were stoned to death" (Prescott. *History of the Conquest of Mexico,* Vol. 1, p. 59).
To the Aztecs adultery was to be avoided and punished (Burland, C.A. *The Gods of Mexico,* p. 101).

1.77 COMMITTING ADULTERY WITH THE "HEART" WAS SINFUL AMONG THE ISRAELITES.

"Lust not after her beauty in thine heart; neither let her take thee with her eyelids" (Proverbs 6:25).

"Eat thou not bread of him that hath an evil eye...For as he thinketh in his heart, so is he..." (Proverbs 23:6-7).

COMMITTING ADULTERY WITH THE "EYES" WAS SINFUL AMONG THE ANCIENT AMERICANS.

"A more extraordinary, coincidence may be traced with Christian rites...But the most striking parallel with (Christian) Scripture is in the remarkable declaration, that 'he who looks too curiously on a woman, commits adultery with his eyes.'" (Prescott. *History of the Conquest of Mexico,* Vol. 1, pp. 84, 85).

1.78 RIGHTEOUS LIVING WAS A MAJOR DOCTRINE OF THE ISRAELITES.

"Let us hear the conclusion of the whole matter, Fear God, and keep his commandments, For this is the whole duty of man. For God shall bring every work into judgment, with every secret thing, whether it be good, or whether it be evil" (Ecclesiastes 12:13-14).

RIGHTEOUS LIVING WAS A MAJOR DOCTRINE OF THE ANCIENT AMERICANS.

"Quetzalcoatl...taught his people science and morality" (Honore. *In Quest of the White God,* p. 16).

The priests of Quetzalcoatl were educated in schools that taught chastity, prudence, reverence and right living. They were taught to shun filth, vice and anything blame-worthy in their lives (Burland, C.A. *The Gods of Mexico,* p. 152).

1.79 ISRAELITES CONFESSED THEIR SINS TO THEIR LEADERS.

"Speak unto the children of Israel, When a man or woman shall commit any sin that men commit, to do a trespass against the LORD, and that person be guilty; Then they shall confess their sin which they have done" (Numbers 5:6-7).

ANCIENT AMERICANS CONFESSED THEIR SINS TO THEIR LEADERS.

"Further, the new rites and doctrine (of Catholicism). had many similarities to their own to commend them to the natives... confession was heard by regular confessors, who extended absolution in the name of the deity concerned" (Bancroft. *History of Mexico,* Vol. 2, p. 182).

1.80 PRAYER WAS PRACTICED BY THE ISRAELITES.

"Evening, and morning, and at noon, will I pray, and cry aloud: and he shall hear my prayer" (Psalms 55:17).

"The LORD is far from the wicked: but he heareth the prayer of the righteous" (Proverbs 15:29).

PRAYER WAS PRACTICED BY THE MAYANS.

"They—the Maya—pray that the eyes of their children may read the writings on the stone tablets" (Makemson. The *Book of the Jaguar Priest [The Book of Chilam Balam of Tizimin], p.* 5, see also p. 9; Burland, C.A. The *Gods of Mexico,* pp. 152-153; Von Hagen, The *Ancient Sun Kingdoms of the Americas,* pp. 435-436).

1.81　**FASTING, THE ABSENCE OF FOOD AND DRINK FOR SPIRITUAL SUPPORT WAS PRACTICED BY THE ISRAELITES.**

"Go, gather together all the Jews that are present in Shushan, and fast ye for me, and neither eat nor drink three days, night or day: I also and my maidens will fast likewise; and so will I go in unto the king, which is not according to the law: and if I perish, I perish" (Esther 4:16).

FASTING, THE ABSENCE OF FOOD AND DRINK FOR SPIRITUAL SUPPORT WAS PRACTICED BY THE ANCIENT AMERICANS.

"As the natives learned more about Catholicism, they found many beliefs and practices in it that were similar to their own...both believed in baptism, confession, fasting..." (Toor. *A Treasury of Mexican Folkways,* p. 104).

Fasting in ancient America is a topic in other books (Nicholson. *Mexican and Central American Mythology,* p. 115; Von Hagen, The *Ancient Sun Kingdoms of the Americas,* pp. 435-436).

1.82　**"HEBREWS" IS A NICKNAME OF THE ISRAELITES GIVEN TO THEM BY FOREIGNERS.**

"Hebrew. This word first occurs as given to Abram by the Canaanites (Genesis 14:13) because he had crossed the Euphrates...The term Israelite was used by the Jews among themselves, the term Hebrew was the name by which they were known to foreigners" (Smith. *Smith's Bible Dictionary,* p. 228).

"INDIANS" IS A NICKNAME OF THE ANCIENT AMERICANS GIVEN TO THEM BY FOREIGNERS.

The American "Indians" were so-named by Europeans when the first transatlantic voyages were made from Europe going to the west, thinking that they were on a new route to India. When they arrived in America and found a race which was not similar to their own, but similar to the race in India, the name was an assumption that their new route was a success, and that they had, in fact, arrived in India; thus they were named Indians by the Europeans.

1.83   ISRAELITES BELIEVED THAT THE FULLNESS OF TRUTH WOULD BE RESTORED TO THE EARTH IN THE LAST DAYS.

"And it shall come to pass in the last days, that the mountain of the LORD'S house shall be established in the top of the mountains, and shall be exalted above the hills; and all nations shall flow unto it" (Isaiah 2:2).

"But there is a God in heaven that revealeth...what shall be in the latter days...the God of heaven set up a kingdom, which shall never be destroyed...and it shall stand for ever" (Daniel 2:28 and 44).

ANCIENT AMERICANS BELIEVED THAT THE FULLNESS OF TRUTH WOULD BE RESTORED TO THE EARTH IN THE LAST DAYS.

"The philosophers and the highest priests knew that the power of Tezcatlipoca would come to an end in the fullness of time, only to be replaced by the more complete worship of Quetzalcoatl" (Burland, C.A. *The Gods of Mexico*, p. 116).

1.84   ISRAELITES BELIEVED THAT IN THE LAST DAYS THE EARTH WILL RETURN BACK TO ITS FIRST ESTATE OF PARADISE—A NEW EARTH.

"For the LORD shall comfort Zion: he will comfort all her waste places; and he will make her wilderness like Eden, and her desert like the garden of the LORD; joy and gladness shall be found therein" (Isaiah 51:3).

THE MAYAS BELIEVED THAT IN THE LAST DAYS THE EARTH WILL RETURN BACK TO ITS FIRST ESTATE OF PARADISE—A NEW EARTH.

"The Mayas envisaged an end when creation would return to its be-ginnings" (Nicholson. *Mexican and Central American Mythology*, p. 20).

HOW CAN WE EXPLAIN THESE PARALLELS?

"And all the evidence slowly coming to light, chronicles and finds, suggested *parallels between the Indians and the Old World* so striking that many writers felt there could be only one explanation: all Indian civilizations must at some time in the dim past have come from the Old World" (Honore. *In Quest of the White God*, p. 70).

And they were Israelites!

Section Two

Israelite Scriptures
Were In
Ancient America

There are several sacred writings of the ancient Americans, such as the *Popol Vuh*, the *Chilam Balam of Chumayel*, the *Chilam Balam of Tizamin*, the *Chilam Balam of Mani*, and the *Teoamaxtli*. Is there any evidence that they also have been influenced by true prophets of God? Do they have similarities with the Bible? The most sacred of those books is, without a doubt, the *Popol Vuh*.

The original *Popol Vuh*, as described by the modern version, is "hidden from the searcher," and thus, not available.

The modern *Popol Vuh* was an attempt, between the years 1554 and 1558, to duplicate from the memories of some wise elderly Mayan priests the sacred book of the Ancient Quiche Maya of the highlands of Guatemala. *Popol Vuh* means "Book of the People."

There are several English versions of the modern *Popol Vuh*. The one used in this study is probably the most popular.

The original *Popol Vuh* is considered by historians as America's oldest book, and its modern version is the most important record that survived the destruction of ancient American records during the Spanish Conquest.

The *Chilam Balam* writings mentioned above came from the Mayan Indians of Yucatan. *Chilam* means "Prophet" and *Balam* means "Jaguar" however, "Balam" is also a family surname in Yucatan.

The similarities between t he Old Testament and the *Popol Vuh* are so obvious that some writers have said:

> "But it seems possible, nonetheless, that they (the Maya) did know the Bible. The parallels are too numerous and striking for mere coincidence (Honore. *In Quest of the White God*. p. 34).

33

"Max Muller had previously (1878) referred to certain similarities between the *Popol Vuh* and the Old Testament, but...he believes that it must be recognized that its content was a true product of the intellectual soil of America" (Goetz and Morley. *Popol Vuh,* p. 19).

But the question is– Where did the American Indians get their similarities with the Bible? Either:

A) They, being lost Israelites, brought the knowledge about the scriptures with them from the Holy Land, or:

B) They were visited by someone who had knowledge about the scriptures, or:

C) They had the knowledge revealed to them by their own prophets.

D) Maybe some or, all of the above.

Whatever the answer is, the fact is: they had abundant knowledge about the Hebrew Scriptures thus, the *Pool Vuh* gives evidence in this Section that there must have been Israelites in America long before the time of Columbus.

The Popol Vuh quotations in this section are reprinted by permission from Popol Vuh: *The Sacred Book of the Ancient Quiche Maya.* English version by Delia Goetz and Sylvanus G. Morley from the translation of Adrian Recinos. Copyright © 1950 by the University of Oklahoma Press, Norman. All Rights Reserved (Invoice No. 4894).

Note: There are many versions of the Bible—I, the author, have thirty-five English versions of the Old Testament and fifty English versions of the New Testament. This section uses three versions to show the various translations used by many major Christian churches.

1. **DOU**—The Douay Version—used by many Catholic churches.

2. **NIV**—The New International Version—used by many Protestant churches.

3. **AKJ**—The Authorized King James Version—used by many Protestant and other churches which are neither Catholic nor Protestant.

2.1. LIVING PROPHETS PRODUCED THE OLD TESTAMENT AND THE NEW TESTAMENT.

"For the Lord God doth nothing without revealing his secret to his servants the prophets" (Amos 3:7 DOU).

"Surely the Sovereign Lord does nothing without revealing his plan to his servants the prophets" (Amos 3:7 NIV).

"Surely the LORD God will do nothing, but he revealeth his secret unto his servants the prophets" (Amos 3:7 AKJ).

LIVING PROPHETS PRODUCED THE POPUL VUH AND OTHER ANCIENT AMERICAN WRITINGS.

The Popul Vuh was full of prophesies and revelations given to their prophets (Goetz and Morley. Popul Vuh, Forward, pp. ix-x and the Introduction, p. 11).

The Books of *Chilam Balam of Chumayel, Chilam Balam of Tizimin, and Chilam Balam of Mani* are three of several sacred books of the Maya of Yucatan. *Chilam* means "Prophet," and *Balam* means "Jaguar," Chumayel, Tizimin and Mani are the names of small towns in Yucatan (Roys. *The Book of Chilam Balam of Chumayel,* p. 3; Makemson. *The Book of the Jaguar Priest* [*The book of Chilam Balam of Tizimin*], pp. 32 and 55).

The big question about this is—were they true prophets or false prophets?

The following similarities should help us get the answer,

2.2. THE GOD OF THE EARTH IN THE BIBLE WAS "ELOHIM."
Throughout the Hebrew scriptures, the chief name for "GOD" was ELOHIM (Smith. *Smith's Bible Dictionary,* p. 212).

THE GOD OF THE EARTH IN THE POPOL VUH WAS "E ALOM."
"Only the Creator, the Maker, Tepeu, Gucumatz, the Forefathers...*E Alom* (Forefathers), literally, those who conceive and give birth" (Goetz and Morley. *Popol Vuh,* p. 81).

2.3. THE BIBLE SAYS THAT THE EARTH WAS CREATED BY MORE THAN ONE CREATOR—THE CREATOR "ELOHIM," IS PLURAL.
"In the beginning God (*Elohim*) created heaven, and earth" (Genesis 1:1 DOU).
"In the beginning God (Elohim) created the heavens and the earth" (Genesis 1:1 NIV).
"In the beginning God (*Elohim*) created the heaven and the earth" (Genesis 1:1 AKJ).
"Elohim is the plural of Eloah (in Arabic: Allah)... " (Smith. *Smith's Bible Dictionary,* p. 212).

A LITERAL TRANSLATION WOULD BE "GODS CREATED."
"And he said, Let us make man in our image and likeness..." (Genesis 1:26 DOU).
"Then God said, Let us make man in our image, in our likeness..." (Genesis 1:26 NIV).
"And God said, Let us make man in our image, after our likeness..." (Genesis 1:26 AKJ).
And also:

"And he said: Behold Adam is become as one of us, knowing good and evil…" (Genesis 3:22 DOU).

"And the LORD God said, The man has now become like one of us, knowing good and evil…" (Genesis 3:22 NIV).

"And the LORD God said, Behold, the man is become as one of us, to know good and evil…" (Genesis 3:22 AKJ).

THE POPOL VUH SAYS THAT THE EARTH WAS CREATED BY MORE THAN ONE CREATOR—THE CREATOR "E ALOM" IS PLURAL.

"Only the Creator, the Maker, Tepeu, Gucumatz, the Forefathers…E Alom (Forefathers), literally, those who conceive and give birth…Then came the word Tepeu and Gucumatz came together…They talked then, discussing and deliberating; they agreed, they united their words and their thoughts. Then while they meditated, it became clear to them that when dawn would break, man must appear…Then the earth was created by them. So it was in truth, that they created the earth" (Goetz and Morley. *Popol Vuh*, pp. 81-83).

2.4.   THE TRINITY, THREE PERSONS UNITED IN THE GODHEAD, ARE IN THE BIBLE.

"And there are Three who give testimony in heaven, the Father, the Word, and the Holy Ghost. And these three are one" (1 John 5:7 DOU).

"For there are three that testify; (1 John 5:7 NIV).

"For there are three that bear record in heaven, the Father, the Word, and the Holy Ghost: and these three are one" (1 John 5:7 AKJ).

THE TRINITY, THREE PERSONS UNITED IN THE GODHEAD, ARE IN THE POPOL VUH.

"In this manner the sky existed and also the Heart of Heaven, which is the name of God and thus He is called…The first (in the Heart of Heaven) is called Caculha-Huracan. The second is Chipi-Caculha. The Third is Raxa-Caculha. And these three are the Heart of Heaven" (Goetz and Morley. *Popol Vuh*, p. 82).

2.5.   THE BIBLICAL ACCOUNT OF THE CREATION OF THE EARTH STARTS WITH "EMPTINESS."

"And the earth was void and empty…" (Genesis 1:2 DOU).

"Now the earth was formless and empty…" (Genesis 1:2 NIV).

"And the earth was without form and void…" (Genesis 1:2 AKJ).

THE POPOL VUH ACCOUNT OF THE CREATION OF THE EARTH STARTS WITH "EMPTINESS."

"…the expanse of the sky was empty…Nothing existed" (Goetz and Morley. *Popol Vuh*, p. 81).

2.6. **THE BIBLICAL ACCOUNT OF THE CREATION OF THE EARTH RECORDS "DARKNESS" WITH THE EMPTINESS.**

"... and darkness was upon the face of the deep..." (and Genesis 1:2 DOU and AKJ).

"... darkness was over the surface of the deep..." (Genesis 1:2 NIV). **THE POPOL VUH ACCOUNT OF THE CREATION OF THE EARTH RECORDS "DARKNESS" WITH THE EMPTINESS.**

"There was only immobility and silence in the darkness, in the night" (Goetz and Morley. *Popol Vuh,* p. 81).

2.7. **AFTER THE DARKNESS OF THE CREATION OF THE EARTH, THE BIBLE SAYS: "LET THERE BE LIGHT."**

"And God said, Be light made. And light was made" (Genesis 1:3 DOU).

"And God said, Let there be light: and there was light (and Genesis 1:3 NIV and AKJ).

AFTER THE DARKNESS OF THE CREATION OF THE EARTH, THE POPOL VUH SAYS: "LET THERE BE LIGHT."

"Let there be light, let there be dawn in the sky and on the earth!" (Goetz and Morley. *Popol* Vuh, p. 83).

2.8. **AFTER THE CREATION OF LIGHT UPON THE EARTH, THE BIBLE RECORDS: "THE WATERS WERE DIVIDED."**

"...Let there be a firmament made amidst the waters: and let it divide the waters from the waters" (Genesis 1:6 DOU).

"...Let there be an expanse between the waters to separate water from water" (Genesis 1:6 NIV).

"...Let there be a firmament in the midst of the waters, and let it divide the waters from the waters" (Genesis 1:6 AKJ).

AFTER THE CREATION OF LIGHT UPON THE EARTH, THE POPOL VUH RECORDS: "THE WATERS WERE DIVIDED."

"...the currents of water were divided, the rivulets were running freely between the hills..." (Goetz and Morley. *Popol Vuh,* p. 84).

2.9. **AFTER THE WATERS WERE DIVIDED THE BIBLE RECORDS: "LET THE DRY LAND APPEAR."**

"...Let the waters under the heaven be gathered together into one place and let the dry land appear. And it was so done" (Genesis 1:9 DOU).

"...Let the water under the sky be gathered to one place, and let dry ground appear" (Genesis 1:9 NIV).

"...Let the waters under the heaven be gathered together unto one place and let the dry land appear. And it was so done" (Genesis 1:9 AKJ).

AFTER THE WATERS WERE DIVIDED, THE POPOL VUH RECORDS: "LET THE EARTH APPEAR."

"Let the water recede and make a void, let the earth appear and become solid" (Goetz and Morley. *Popol Vuh*, p. 83).

2.10. **THE BIBLE SAYS THAT THE CREATION WAS VERY GOOD.**

"And God saw all the things that he had made and, they were very good..." (Genesis 1:31 DOU).

"God saw all that he had made, and it was very good..." (Genesis 1:31 NIV).

"And God saw that every thing that he had made and, behold, it was yew good..." (Genesis 1:31 AKJ).

THE POPOL VUH SAYS THAT THE CREATION WAS PERFECT.

"So it was that they made perfect the work, when they did it after thinking and meditating upon it" (Goetz and Morley. *Popol Vuh*, p. 84).

2.11. **THE BIBLE DECLARES THAT THE CREATION OF THE EARTH WAS FINISHED.**

"So the heavens and the earth were finished, and all the furniture of them" (Genesis 2:1 DOU).

"Thus the heavens and the earth were completed in all their vast array" (Genesis 2:1 NIV).

"Thus, the heavens and the earth were finished, and all the host of them" (Genesis 2:1 AKJ).

THE POPOL VUH DECLARES THAT THE CREATION OF THE EARTH WAS FINISHED.

"Then the earth was created by them. So it was, in truth, that they created the earth" (Goetz and Morley. *Popol Vuh*, p. 83).

2.12. **IN THE BIBLE, GOD TELLS THE ANIMALS AND BIRDS TO "MULTIPLY."**

"And God created the great whales, and every living and moving creature...and every winged fowl according to his kind...And he blessed them, saying: Increase and multiply..." (Genesis 1:21-22 DOU).

"So God created the great creatures of the sea and every living and moving thing...and every winged bird according to its kind...God blessed them and said, Be fruitful, and increase..." (Genesis 1:21-22 NIV).

"And God created great whales, and every living creature that moveth...and every winged fowl after his kind...And God blessed them, saying, Be fruitful, and multiply..." (Genesis 1:21-22 AKJ).

IN THE POPOL VUH, GOD TELLS THE ANIMALS AND BIRDS TO "MULTIPLY."

"...to the deer and the birds...in the woods you shall multiply..." (Goetz and Morley. *Popol Vuh*, p. 85).

2.13. THE BIBLE SAYS THE ANIMALS WERE MADE "AFTER THEIR OWN KIND."

"And God said: Let the earth bring forth the living creature in its kind, cattle, and creeping things, and beasts of the earth according to their kinds. And it was so done. And God made the beasts of the earth according to their kinds, and cattle and everything that creepeth upon the earth after its kind..." (Genesis 1:24-25 DOU).

"And God said, Let the land produce living creatures according to their kinds, cattle, and creeping thing, and beast of the earth after his kind: and it was so. And God made the beast of the earth after his kind, and cattle after their kind, and everything that creepeth upon the earth after his kind..." (Genesis 1:24-25 NIV).

"And God said, Let the earth bring forth the living creature after his kind, cattle, and creeping thing, and beast of the earth after his kind: and it was so. And God made the beast of the earth after his kind, and cattle after their kind, and everything that creepeth upon the earth after his kind..." (Genesis 1:24-25 AKJ).

THE POPOL VUH SAYS THE ANIMALS WERE MADE "AFTER THEIR OWN KIND."

"Then they made the small wild animals, the guardians of the woods, the spirits of mountains, the deer, the birds, pumas, jaguars, serpents, snakes...each according to your variety, each according our kind" (Goetz and Morley. *Popol Vuh*, pp. 84-85).

2.14. THE BIBLE SAYS THAT MAN WAS CREATED BY MORE THAN ONE PERSON.

"And he said: Let us make man in our image and likeness...and the evening and morning were the sixth day" (Genesis 1:26-31 DOU).

"Then God said, Let us make man in our image, in our likeness...And there was an evening, and there was a morning the sixth day" (Genesis 1:26-31 NIV).

"And God said, Let us make man in our image, after our likeness...and the evening and morning were the sixth day" (Genesis 1:26-31 AKJ).

THE POPOL VUH SAYS THAT MAN WAS CREATED BY MORE THAN ONE PERSON.

"Then while they meditated, it became clear to them that when dawn would break, man must appear. Then they planned the creation...of life and the creation of man" (Goetz and Morley. *Popol Vuh,* p. 82).

2.15.   THE BIBLE SAYS THAT MAN WAS MADE FROM THE EARTH.

"And the Lord God formed man of the slime of the earth..." (Genesis 2:7 DOU).

"...the Lord God formed the man from the dust of the ground..." (Genesis 2:7 NIV).

"And the Lord God formed man from the dust of the ground..." (Genesis 2:7 AKJ).

THE POPOL VUH SAYS THAT MAN WAS MADE FROM THE EARTH.

"Of earth, of mud, they made (man's) flesh" (Goetz and Morley. *Popol Vuh,* p. 86).

2.16.   THE BIBLE ACCOUNT OF THE CREATION SAYS THAT, UNLIKE THE ANIMALS, MAN WAS RELATED TO THE CREATORS.

"And he said: Let us make man in our image and likeness...And God created man to his own image; to the image of God he created him..." (Genesis 1:26-27 DOU).

"Then God said, Let us make man in our image, in our likeness...So God created man in his own image, in the image of God he created him..." (Genesis 1:26-27 NIV).

"And God said, Let us make man in our image, after our likeness...So God created man in his own image, in the image of God created he him..." (Genesis 1:26-27 AKJ).

THE POPOL VUH ACCOUNT OF THE CREATION SAYS THAT, UNLIKE THE ANIMAL, MAN WAS RELATED TO THE CREATORS.

"Let us make him (man) who shall nourish and sustain us...So then let us try to make obedient and respectful beings who will nourish and sustain us" (Goetz and Morley. *Popol Vuh.* p. 86).

"Only the Creator, the Maker, Tepeu, Gucumatz, the Foreththers. E Alom, literally, those who conceive and give birth" (Goetz and Morley. *Popol Vuh.* pp. 81).

2.17. **AFTER THE CREATION THE BIBLE TELLS OF A SATANIC PERSON WITH A FRUITFUL TREE.**

Lucifer, in the form of a serpent, praised the forbidden tree in the midst of the garden of Eden and tried to get Eve to partake of its fruit (Genesis 3:1-4).

AFTER THE CREATION THE POPOL VUH TELLS OF A SATANIC PERSON WITH A FRUITFUL TREE.

"Vucub-Caquix (a satanic person) had a large Nantze tree*...Each day he were to the tree and climbed to the top" (Goetz and Morley. *Popol Vuh*, p. 96).

(*Byrsonima Continifolia, B. Crassifolia,* a beautiful tropical tree which produces a very aromatic fruit similar to the white cherry)" and

2.18. **THE BIBLE SAYS A WOMAN WAS TEMPTED TO PICK SOME FRUIT FROM A TREE THAT WOULD CAUSE HER TO DIE.**

"But of the fruit of the tree which is in the midst of paradise, God hath commanded us that we should not eat: and that we should not touch it, lest perhaps we die. And the serpent said to the woman: No you shall not die the death" (Genesis 3:3-4 DOU).

"...but God did say, You must not eat fruit from the tree that is in the middle of the garden, and you must not touch it, or ye will die. You will not surely die, the serpent said to the woman" (Genesis 3:3-4 NIV).

"But of the fruit of the tree which is in the midst of the garden, God hath said, Ye shall not eat of it, neither shall ye touch it, lest ye die. And the serpent said unto the woman, Ye shall not surely die" (Genesis 3:3-4 AKJ).

THE POPOL VUH SAYS A WOMAN WAS TEMPTED TO PICK SOME FRUIT FROM A TREE THAT WOULD CAUSE HER TO DIE.

"'Ah!' she exclaimed, 'What fruit is this which this tree bears? Is it not wonderful to see how it is covered with fruit? Must I die, shall I be lost, if I pick one of this fruit?' said the maiden" (Goetz and Morley. *Popol Vuh*, p. 119).

2.19. **THE BIBLE TELLS ABOUT THE GREAT FLOOD THAT COVERED THE EARTH.**

"And the waters prevailed beyond measure upon the earth: and all the high mountains under the whole heaven, were covered...And all flesh was destroyed that moved upon the earth, both of fowl, and of cattle, and of beasts, and of all creeping things that creep upon the earth: and all men...And Noe only remained, and they that were with him in the ark" (Genesis 7:19-23 DOU).

"They rose greatly on the earth; and all the high mountains, under the entire heavens were covered...Every living thing that moved on the earth perished—birds, livestock, wild animals, all the creatures that swarm over the earth, and all mankind.... Only Noah was left, and those with him in the ark" (Genesis 7:19-23 NIV).

"And the waters prevailed exceedingly upon the earth; and all the high hills, that were under the whole heaven, were covered...And all flesh died that moved upon the earth, both of fowl, and of cattle, and of beast, and of every creeping thing that creepeth upon the earth, and every man...and Noah only remained alive, and they that were with him in the ark" (Genesis 7:19-23 AKJ).

THE POPOL VUH TELLS ABOUT THE GREAT FLOOD THAT COVERED THE EARTH.

"A Flood was brought about by the Heart of Heaven; a great flood was formed...But those that they had made, that they had created...were killed, they were deluged" (Goetz and Morley. *Popol Vuh,* p. 90).

2.20.   THE BIBLE SAYS THAT THE GREAT FLOOD CAME BECAUSE OF THE WICKEDNESS OF MAN.

"And God seeing that the wickedness of men was great on the earth, and that all the thoughts of their heart was bent upon evil at all times...He said, I will destroy man, whom I have created, upon the face of the earth..." (Genesis 6:5-7 DOU).

"The LORD saw how great man's wickedness on the earth had become, and that every inclination of the thoughts of his heart was only evil all the time...So the LORD said, I will wipe mankind whom I have created from the face of the earth..." (Genesis 6:5-7 NIV).

"And God saw that the wickedness of man was great in the earth, and that every imagination of the thoughts of his heart was only evil continually...And the LORD said, I will destroy man whom I have created..." (Genesis 6:5-7 AKJ).

THE POPOL VUH SAYS THAT THE GREAT FLOOD CAME BECAUSE OF THE WICKEDNESS OF MAN.

"...they no longer thought of their Creator nor their Maker, nor of those who made them and cared for them. These were the first men who existed in great numbers on the face of the earth...But those that they had made, that they had created, did not think, did not speak with their Creator, their Maker. And for this reason they were killed, they were deluged" (Goetz and Morley. *Popol Vuh,* pp. 89-90).

2.21. **THE BIBLE TELLS ABOUT THE PARTING OF THE SEA AND THE TRIBES WHO CROSSED THE SEA ON DRY GROUND.**

"And when Moses had stretched forth his hand over the sea, the LORD took it away by a strong and burning wind blowing all the night: and turned it into dry ground, and the water was divided. And the children of Israel went in through the midst of the sea dried up: for the water was as a wall on their right hand, and on their left" (Exodus 14:21-22 DOU).

"Then Moses stretched forth his hand over the sea. And all that night the LORD drove the sea back with a strong east wind and turned it into dry land. The waters were divided, and the Israelites went through the sea on the dry ground, with a wall of water on their right and on their left" (Exodus 14:21-22 NIV).

"And Moses stretched forth his hand over the sea; and the LORD caused the sea to go back by a strong east wind all that night, and made the sea dry land, and the waters were divided. And the children of Israel went into the midst of the sea upon the dry ground: and the waters were wall unto them on their right hand, and on their left" (Exodus 14:21-22 AKJ).

THE POPOL VUH TELLS ABOUT THE PARTING OF THE SEA AND THE TRIBES WHO CROSSED THE SEA ON DRY GROUND.

"It is not quite clear, however, how they crossed the sea; they crossed to this side, as if there were no sea...they crossed the sea, the waters having parted when they passed" (Goetz and Morley. *Popol Vuh*, p. 183).

2.22. **THE BIBLE SAYS THAT AFTER THE WATERS WERE PARTED, STONES WERE LOCATED WHERE THEY CROSSED THE WATER.**

"That it may be a sign among you: and when your children ask you tomorrow saying, What mean these stones? You shall answer them: The waters of the Jordan ran off before the ark of the covenant of the LORD, when it passed over the same, Therefore were these stones set for a monument of the children of Israel for ever. The children of Israel therefore did as Josue commanded them, carrying out of the channel twelve stones, as the LORD had commanded him, according to the number of the children of Israel..." (Joshua 4:6-8 DOU).

"To serve as a sign among you. In the future, when your children ask you, What do these stones mean? tell them that the flow of Jordan was cut off before the ark of the covenant of the LORD. When it crossed the Jordan, the waters of the Jordan were cut off, These stones are to be a memorial to the people of Israel for ever. So the Israelites did as Joshua commanded them. They took twelve stones from the middle of the Jordan, according to the number of the tribes of the Israelites, as the LORD had told Joshua..." (Joshua 4:6-8 NIV).

"That this may be a sign among you, that when your children ask their fathers in time to come, saying, What mean ye by these stones? Then ye shall answer them, That the waters of Jordan were cut off before the ark of the covenant of the LORD; when it passed over Jordan, the waters of Jordan were cut off: and these stones shall be for a memorial unto the children of Israel for ever. And the children of Israel did so as Joshua commanded, and took up twelve stones out of the midst of Jordan, as the LORD spake unto Joshua, according to the number of the tribes of the children of Israel..." (Joshua 4:6-8 AKJ).

THE POPOL VUH SAYS THAT AFTER THE WATERS WERE PARTED, STONES WERE LOCATED WHERE THEY CROSSED THE WATER.

"It is not quite clear, however, how they crossed the sea; they crossed to this side, as if there were no sea; they crossed on stones, placed in a row over the sand. For this reason they were called Stones in a Row, Sand Under the Sea, names given to them when they (the tribes) crossed the sea, the waters having parted when they passed" (Goetz and Morley. *Popol Vuh*, p. 183).

2.23. **SACRED SEER STONES WERE USED IN THE BIBLE.**

"And thou shalt put in the rational of judgment, *doctrine* and *truth*, which shall be on Aaron's breast..." (Exodus 28:30 DOU, the word stones were not used in this version).

"Also put the Urim and Thurnmim in the breastpiece, so they may be over Aaron's heart..." (Exodus 28:30 NIV).

"And thou shalt put in the breastplate of judgment the Urim and the Thummim; and they shall be upon Aaron's heart..." (Exodus 28:30 AKJ).

"In what way the Urim and Thummim were consulted is quite uncertain. Josephus and the Rabbins supposed that the stones gave out the oracular answer by preternatural illumination" (Smith. *Smith's Bible Dictionary*, p. 719).

SACRED SEER STONES WERE USED IN THE POPOL VUH.

"Tohil, Avilix, and Hacavitz had the appearance of three youths and walked by virtue of the magic stone" (Goetz and Morley. *Popol Vuh*, p. 195).

2.24. **CONSTANT REVELATION FROM GOD WAS NECESSARY TO PROPERLY GUIDE THE EARLY ISRAELITES.**

"When prophesy shall fall, the people shall be scattered abroad..." (Proverbs 29:18 DOU).

"Where there is no revelation, the people cast off restraint" (Proverbs 29:18 NIV).

"Where there is no vision, the people perish" (Proverbs 29:18 AKJ). **CONSTANT REVELATION FROM GOD WAS NECESSARY TO PROPERLY GUIDE THE EARLY AMERICANS.**

"...a chosen people who are able to speak for the gods was characteristic of Maya and Nahua religion...we regard it as representing revelation from a high source" (Nicholson. *Mexican and Central American Mythology*, p. 15, see also p.107).

The Popul Vuh was the most sacred book of the Ancient Quiche Maya. It was full of prophesies and revelations given to their Prophets (Goetz and Morley. Popul Vuh, p. ix).

2.25.   **THE FIVE BOOKS OF MOSES IN THE BIBLE CONTAIN HISTORY, CEREMONIES, REVELATIONS, NAMES OF CHILDREN OF ISRAEL AND MARRIAGE RITES.**

A)   Genesis contains the history of the Patriarchs and their ages and time (Genesis 5-50).

B)   Exodus contains the deliverance of Israel out of bondage, their ceremonies and feast days (Exodus 17-40).

C)   Leviticus contains revelations and auguries (prophesies) and some ancient requirements (Leviticus 11-15).

D)   Numbers contains the way the children of Israel were named and numbered into tribes (Numbers 1-4).

E)   Deuteronomy contains warnings of marriage rites with the Canaanites (Deuteronomy 7), plural marriage rites (Deuteronomy 17) and divorces (Deuteronomy 24).

FIVE BOOKS OF MEXICAN INDIANS CONTAIN HISTORY, CEREMONIES, DREAMS, NAMES OF CHILDREN AND MARRIAGE RITES; AS DESCRIBED IN THE INTRODUCTION OF THE MODERN POPOL VUH.

"Bishop Las Casas reports that the Mexican Indians had five books of figures and characters."

A)   "The first book contained the history and the computation of their time."

B)   "...the second (book) had the days of ceremony and the feast days of each year...."

C)   "...the third (book) dealt with dreams, auguries, and superstitions...."

D)   "...the fourth (book) with the way in which children were named..."

E)   "...the fifth contained their marriage rites and ceremonies" (Goetz and Morley. *Popol Vuh*, p. 8).

2.26. THE BIBLE EMPHASIZES THE WARS, VICTORIES, DEFEATS, AND CONQUESTS OF THE ISRAELITES.

Moses prophesied of Israel's future wars, victories, and defeats, and conquest in Canaan (Deuteronomy 7). Israel is victorious in the war with Jericho (Joshua 6). Israel is defeated by the people of Ai (Joshua 7). Israel conquers the whole land of Canaan (Joshua 11).

THE FIVE BOOKS OF THE MEXICAN INDIANS EMPHASIZE THE WARS, VICTORIES, DEFEATS, AND CONQUESTS OF THEIR PEOPLE.

"He (Bishop Las Casas) adds that...the books of the first class told of their wars, victories, and defeats...and their conquests..." (Goetz and Morley. *Popol Vuh*, p. 8).

2.27. THE FIVE BOOKS OF MOSES EMPHASIZE THE ORIGIN, GENEALOGY AND DEEDS OF THEIR PRINCIPAL LORDS.

Genesis tells of the origin, and genealogy of Israel (Genesis 9-11), and the deeds of the principal lords, Abraham, Isaac Jacob, and Joseph (Genesis 11-50).

THE FIVE BOOKS OF THE MEXICAN INDIANS EMPHASIZE THE ORIGIN, GENEALOGY AND DEEDS OF THEIR PRINCIPAL LORDS.

"He (Bishop Las Casas) adds that...the books of the first class told of their...origin, genealogy, and deeds of the principal lords..." (Goetz and Morley. *Popol Vuh*, p. 8).

2.28. THE "DEVIL" OF THE BIBLE WANTS PEOPLE TO WORSHIP HIM.

"Again the devil took him up into a very high mountain, and shewed him all the kingdoms of the world and the glory of them, And said to him: All these will give thee, if falling down thou wilt adore me" (Matthew 4:8-9 DOU).

"Again, the devil took him to a very high mountain and showed him all the kingdoms of the world and their splendor. 'All this I will give you.' He said, 'if you will bow down and worship me" (Matthew 4:8-9 NIV).

"Again, the devil taketh him up into an exceeding high mountain, and sheweth him all the kingdoms of the world, and the glory of them; And saith unto him, All these things will I give thee, if you wilt fall down and worship me" (Matthew 4:8-9 AKJ).

THE "DEVIL" OF THE POPOL VUH WANTS PEOPLE TO WORSHIP HIM.

"'I shall now be great above all the beings created and formed, I am the sun, the light, the moon,' he exclaimed. 'Great is my splendor, Because of me men shall walk and conquer...' (Vucub-Caquix, that is to say, Seven Macaws, Ximenez believed he saw in this personage a kind of Lucifer...). His only ambition was to exalt himself and to dominate" (Goetz and Morley. *Popol Vuh,* pp. 93, 94).

2.29. THE OLD TESTAMENT WAS ORIGINALLY WRITTEN IN HEBREW.

The Old Testament is called "The Hebrew Scriptures," since the original manuscripts were written in Hebrew.

SOME ANCIENT AMERICAN BOOKS WERE WRITTEN IN CHARACTERS WHICH RESEMBLED HEBREW.

"... the Spaniards, during their expedition of 1696 against the Itza, found some books written with characters which resembled Hebrew characters" (Goetz and Morley. *Popol Vuh,* pp. 10-11).

2.30. THE BIBLE CONTAINS PROPHECIES OF GOD.

"And they came to the foresaid hill, and behold a company of prophets met him. And the Spirit of the Lord came upon him, and he prophesied in the midst of them" (1 Samuel 10:10 DOU).

"When they arrived at Gibeah, a procession of prophets met him; the Spirit of God came upon him in power, and he joined in their prophesying" (1 Samuel 10:10 NIV).

"And when they came thither to the hill, behold, a company of prophets met him; and the Spirit of God came upon him, and he prophesied among them" (1 Samuel 10:10 AKJ).

The Bible is full of prophesies, written by Prophets.

THE POPOL VUH CONTAINS PROPHECIES OF GOD.

"The *Popol Vuh* was also the book of prophesies and the oracle of the kings and the lords..." (Goetz and Morley, *Popol Vuh,* p. 19).

"... the Spaniards, during their expedition of 1696 against the Itza, found some books written with characters which resembled Hebrew... contained prophecies of future events...which their gods announced to them" (Goetz and Morley. *Popol Vuh,* pp. 10-11).

2.31. THE BIBLE SAYS THAT SOME ISRAELITES WERE SENT IN EVERY DIRECTION ON EARTH.

"And thy (Jacob's) seed shall be as the dust of the earth: Thou shalt spread abroad to the west, and to the east, and to the north, and to the south; and in thee and my seed all the tribes of the earth shall be blessed" (Genesis 28:14 DOU).

"Your (Jacob's) descendants will be like the dust of the earth, and you will spread out to the west and to the east, to the north and to the south. All peoples on earth will be blessed through you and your offspring" (Genesis 28:14 NIV).

"And thy (Jacob's) seed shall be as the dust of the earth, and thou shalt spread abroad to the west, and to the east, and to the north, and to the south; and in thee and in thy seed shall all the families of the earth be blessed" (AKJ Genesis 28:14).

THE POPOL VUH SAYS THAT THE ANCIENT AMERICANS CAME ACROSS THE ATLANTIC OCEAN.

"Sahagun is very explicit when he says *(Historia general de las cosas de Nueva Espana* [1938 ed.] Book X. Chap. XXIX) that the first inhabitants of New Spain (America) landed in Panutla (Panuco, the Gulf of Mexico coast)" (Goetz and Morley. *Popol Vuh,* p. 77, see also pp. 14 and 38). Many ancient American traditions tell us that many came by boat, from the east, on the Atlantic side of America (Burland, C.A. *The Gods of Mexico,* pp. 185, 186; Willard. *The City of the Sacred Well,* pp. 34, 35).

2.32. THE OLD TESTAMENT TELLS OF THE CREATION OF THE EARTH, THE EMIGRATIONS AND JOURNEYS OF GOD'S PEOPLE, THEIR KINGS, RELIGIOUS PRACTICES, THEIR SONGS AND POETRY.

Genesis records the creation of the earth.

Exodus records migrations and journeys of the Israelites.

Leviticus, Numbers, and Deuteronomy records the history of their stopping places

1 Kings and 2 Kings record the dynasties of their kings.

Ruth, Ezra, Nehemiah and Esther record their social and religious practices.

.Psalms, Proverbs, and Song of Solomon record songs and poetry.

THE TOLTECS' DIVINE BOOK IS VERY SIMILAR TO THE OLD TESTAMENT.

"According to Ixtlilxochitl, Huematzin, the king of Tezcuco, had gathered together all the chronicles of the Tolteca in the *Teoamoxtli,* or Divine Book, which contained the legends of the creation of the world, the emigration from Asia of those peoples, the stops on the journey, the dynasty of their kings, their social and religious institutions, their sciences, arts, and so on" (Goetz and Morley. *Popol Vuh,* p. 9).

YES—ISRAELITE SCRIPTURES WERE IN ANCIENT AMERICA!

Section Three

Christians
Were in
Ancient America

The similarities between the Israelites and ancient Americans give good evidence that Christ would want to visit his chosen people in America. If he did visit them, then there should be more evidence of that visit by finding some Christian characteristics in the American-Indian history before Columbus.

> When Hernando Cortez was exploring America in 1519, "he was amazed by the sight of a cross, of stone and lime, about ten palms high...it must be regarded as a curious fact, that the cross should have been venerated as an object of religious worship both in the New World, and in the regions of the Old, where the light of Christianity had never risen" (Prescott. *History of the Conquest of Mexico,* Vol. 1, pp. 254-255).

WERE CHRISTIANS IN AMERICA
BEFORE COLUMBUS?

Jesus told his apostles:
"Go ye therefore, and teach all nations...teaching them to observe all things whatsoever I have commanded you" (Matthew 28:19-20).
"And he said unto them, Go ye into all the world, and preach the gospel to every creature" (Mark 16:15).
And again Luke said:

> "... repentance and remission of sins should be preached in his (Jesus') name among all nations, beginning at Jerusalem" (Luke 24:47).

There are many professional and non-professional writers of the myths and traditions of the American Indians that have come to the conclusion that Christianity was definitely taught and practiced in America many centuries before Columbus:

> "We...consider it sufficiently demonstrated that the Christian religion was preached in America during the first centuries of our era" (DeRoo. *America before Columbus*, p. 582).

Many writers have noticed the similarities between Maya traditions and the Christian scriptures (Nicholson. *Mexican and Central American Mythology*, p. 21; Toor. *A Treasury of Mexican Folkways*, p. 104).

THERE ARE TWO MAIN THEORIES OF HOW CHRISTIANITY CAME TO ANCIENT AMERICA.

THEORY NUMBER ONE:
ST. THOMAS, OR ONE OF THE OTHER APOSTLES, VISITED AMERICA AND TAUGHT CHRISTIANITY.

> The Apostles were told by Jesus to "Go ye into all the world, and preach the gospel to every creature" (Mark 16:15).

The Apostle Thomas fits some of the evidences of how the Ancient Americans knew about many Christian doctrines and practices.

> "Quetzalcoatl signifies 'feathered serpent,' the last syllable means, likewise, a 'twin,' which furnishes an argument for Dr. Siguenza to identify this god with the apostle Thomas (Didymous signifying also a twin)" (Prescott. *History of the Conquest of Mexico*, Vol. 1, p. 81).

> "Later divines have found in these teachings of the Toltec god, or high priest, the gems of some of the great mysteries of the Christian faith, as those of the Incarnation, and the Trinity, for example...In the teacher himself, they recognize no less a person than St. Thomas, the Apostle" (Prescott. *History of the Conquest of Mexico*, Vol. 2, p. 5,).

Other writers also express this theory (See: Nicholson. *Mexican and Central American Mythology,* p. 14; Glaser. *Indians or Jews?* p. 11).

THEORY NUMBER TWO:
JESUS CHRIST HIMSELF VISITED AMERICA AFTER HIS RESURRECTION AND TAUGHT HIS GOSPEL.

Jesus told his disciples:
"And other sheep I have, which are not of this fold: them also I must bring, and they shall hear my voice; and there shall be one fold, and one shepherd" (John 10: 16).

Some believe that "his other sheep that would hear his voice" were the Gentiles, but he very clearly said that he was not sent to the Gentiles:

"... I am not sent but unto the lost sheep of the House of Israel" (Matthew 15:24).

"Peru was earlier a center of a good deal of speculation. La Vega comments on it, as does Gieza de Leon. The latter writing of the Peruvian god Tici-Viracocha (another name for Quetzalcoatl), who did have a Christ-like career...'" (Glaser. *Indians or Jews?* p. 11).

The major evidences for this theory are the numberless parallels that exist in the lives of Jesus and Quetzalcoatl, the bearded white god of the Aztecs, many of which are described in section four herein.

Whichever theory is right, the following parallels prove that it is very obvious that Christianity was taught in America long before the arrival of Columbus and the Spaniards, either by Jesus or an Apostle, or both.

3.1.   THE CHRISTIANS BELIEVED IN ONE SUPREME GOD.
"In the beginning was the Word, and the Word was with God, and the Word was God" (John 1:1).
A literal translation of the underlined is:
"...the Word was with θεόν and the Word was θεός (Berry. *The Interlinear Greek - English New Testament,* p. 240, and *Greek-English Lexicon* p. 46).
θεόν means **Theo** = the Supreme God and,
θεός means **Theos** = the subordinate God.
"And the Word was made flesh, and dwelt among us..." (John 1:14).
Yes – the Word was Jesus.
"...I (Jesus) go unto the father: for my Father is greater than I" (John 14:28, 5:19 and 7:16).

"But I would have you know, that the head of every man is Christ...and the head of Christ is God (Theo)" (1 Corinthians 11:3).

SOME ANCIENT AMERICANS BELIEVED IN ONE SUPREME GOD.

"The Aztecs recognized the existence of a supreme Creator and Lord of the universe. They addressed him, in their prayers, as 'God by whom we live.' 'omnipresent, that knoweth all thoughts, and giveth all gifts.' 'without whom a man is as nothing,' 'invisible, incorporeal, one God, of perfect perfection and purity'" (Prescott. *History of the Conquest of Mexico,* Vol. 1, p. 78).

The Aztecs spoke about Ometeo the great god above all (Nicholson. *Mexican and Central American Mythology,* p. 114-115).

3.2. CHRISTIANS BELIEVED THEY WERE CHILDREN OF GOD.

"Be ye therefore perfect, even as your Father which is in heaven is perfect" (Matthew 5:48).

"After this manner therefore pray he: Our Father which art in heaven, Hallowed be thy name" (Matthew 6:9).

"Forasmuch then as we are the offspring of God, we ought not to think that the Godhead is like unto gold, or silver, or stone, graven by art and man's device" (Acts 17:29).

SOME ANCIENT AMERICANS BELIEVED THEY WERE CHILDREN OF GOD.

"... the Lord of Sustenance...automatically becomes associated with human procreation...from this latter god we can derive the transfigurations Two Lord and Two Lady, the gods in the thirteenth heaven who send children down to earth to be born" (Brundage. *The Fifth Sun,* p. 54).

3.3. THE CHRISTIANS CONSIDERED THE CHILDREN OF GOD ON EARTH THAT ACCEPT THE WORD OF GOD TO BE "GODS."

"... Is it not written in your law, I said, Ye are gods? If he called them gods, unto whom the word of God came, and the scripture cannot be broken" (John 10:34-35).

"... we are the children of God: And if children, then heirs; heirs of God, and joint-heirs with Christ..." (Romans 8:16-17).

"Beloved, now are we the sons of God...when he shall appear, we shall be like him; for we shall see him as he is" (1 John 3:2).

The interpretation of these scriptures varies among modern Christians. Many Christians believe they are *potential gods.*

THE AZTECS CONSIDERED THE CHILDREN OF GOD ON EARTH THAT ACCEPT THE WORD OF GOD TO BE "GODS."

"All was joy in this world until the gods (the Aztec Adam and Eve) unaccountably defied the injunction of the Lord of Sustenance...For this breach of the divine command the gods were cast down out of Tamoanchan (garden of Eden).... Oxomoco (the Aztec Eve) being at this point identified as the goddess Obsidian Knife Butterfly" (Brundage. *The Fifth Sun,* pp. 46, 47).

3.4. **CHRISTIANS BELIEVED THEY HAD A PRE-MORTAL LIFE BEFORE THEY WERE BORN ON EARTH.**

"Blessed be the God and Father of our Lord Jesus Christ, who hath blessed us with all spiritual blessings in heavenly places in Christ, According as he hath chosen us in him before the foundation of the earth, that we should be holy..." (Ephesians 1:3-4).

SOME ANCIENT AMERICANS BELIEVED THEY HAD A PRE-MORTAL LIFE BEFORE THEY WERE BORN ON EARTH.

"... the Lord of Sustenance...automatically becomes associated with human procreation...from this latter god we can derive the transfigurations Two Lord and Two Lady, the gods in the thirteenth heaven who send children down to earth to be born" (Brundage. *The Fifth Sun,* p. 54).

Ancient Americans talked about a "first space," or the "first time" outside material creation (Nicholson. *Mexican and Central American Mythology,* p. 21).

3.5. **SATAN, THE DEVIL OF THE CHRISTIANS, WAS CAST OUT OF HEAVEN.**

"And there was a war in heaven: Michael and his angels fought against the dragon; and the dragon fought and his angels, And prevailed not; neither was their place found any more in heaven. And the great dragon was cast out, that old serpent, called the Devil, and Satan, which deceiveth the whole world: he was cast out into the earth, and his angels were cast out with him" (Revelation 12:7-9).

TEZCATLIPOCA, THE DEVIL OF THE ANCIENT AMERICANS, WAS CAST OUT OF HEAVEN.

"Then there is the myth of Tezcatlipoca's fall from heaven. Here we are told that he had sinned and, like Lucifer, was hurled down from the ambrosial regions" (Brundage. *The Fifth Sun,* p. 94, also see pp. 95).

Other writers say Tezcatlipoca fell from heaven, and others say seven devils called "satai," came from heaven. (Makemson. *The Book of the*

Jaguar Priest, p. 35; Nicholson. *Mexican and Central American Mythology,* pp. 98 and 109).

3.6. **THE SPIRIT OF MAN PUTS LIFE INTO THE BODY OF MAN, ACCORDING TO DOCTRINE OF THE CHRISTIANS.**

"For as the body without the spirit is dead, so faith without works is dead also" (James 2:24-26).

THE SPIRIT OF MAN PUTS LIFE INTO THE BODY OF MAN, ACCORDING TO DOCTRINE OF SOME ANCIENT AMERICANS.

"... spirit must enter matter to infuse it with life" (Nicholson. *Mexican and Central American Mythology,* p. 89).

3.7. **THE CHRISTIANS BELIEVED THEY WERE THE CHOSEN PEOPLE OF GOD.**

"But ye are a chosen generation, a royal priesthood, an holy nation, a peculiar people; that ye should shew forth the praises of him who hath called you out of darkness into his marvelous light" (1 Peter 2:9).

SOME ANCIENT AMERICANS BELIEVED THEY WERE THE CHOSEN PEOPLE OF GOD.

Nahua, the name of the people in the central Mexican plateau, means "one who speaks with authority," because they were a chosen people who spoke for the gods (Nicholson. *Mexican and Central American Mythology,* p. 15).

3.8. **THE CHRISTIANS BELIEVED THEY HAD THE POWER OF GOD, DIVINE AUTHORITY TO PERFORM IN HIS NAME.**

"Then he called his twelve disciples together, and gave them power and authority over all devils, and to cure diseases" (Luke 9:1).

SOME ANCIENT AMERICANS BELIEVED THEY HAD THE POWER OF GOD, DIVINE AUTHORITY TO PERFORM IN HIS NAME.

Nahua, the name of the people in the central Mexican plateau, means "one who speaks with authority," because they were a chosen people who spoke for the gods (Nicholson. *Mexican and Central American Mythology,* p. 15).

3.9. **THE PRIESTHOOD, A BROTHERHOOD WITH DIVINE AUTHORITY TO TEACH AND MINISTER TO THE PEOPLE OF GOD, WAS AMONG THE CHRISTIANS.**

"And when he had called unto him his twelve disciples, he gave them power..." (Matthew 10:1).

"But ye are a chosen generation, a royal priesthood, an holy nation, a peculiar people..." (1 Peter 2:9).

THE PRIESTHOOD, A BROTHERHOOD WITH DIVINE AUTHORITY TO TEACH AND MINISTER TO THE PEOPLE OF GOD, WAS AMONG SOME ANCIENT AMERICANS.

Quetzalcoatl, the creator of all things on earth, had his own priesthood (Brundage. *The Fifth sun,* p. 123).

References to "priests," "priestly order," "and "priesthood" are abundant in the writings about ancient America (Burland, C.A., *The Gods of Mexico,* pp. x, 37, 57, 64, 66, 70, 78, 93, 95, 116, 131 and152-and154; Brundage. *The Fifth Sun,* pp. 114-115; and Honore, Pierre. *In Quest of the White God,* p. 34; Makemson, Maud Worcester. *The Book of The Jaguar Priest, The Book of Chilam Balam of Tizimin,* p. 15; Nicholson. *Mexican and Central American Mythology,* pp. 15, 78-79, 83, 120 and 131-132; and Prescott, William H. *History of the Conquest of Mexico,* Vol. 2, p. 5; Roys, Ralph L. *The Book of Chilam Balam of Chumayel,* p. 133; Toor. Frances, *A Treasury of Mexican Folkways,* pp. xxiv and 104).

3.10.　**CRUCIFIXION, INCLUDING BREAKING THE LEGS OF THE VICTIMS, WAS PRACTICED AT JERUSALEM.**

"Then delivered he him therefore unto them to be crucified...The Jews therefore, because it was the preparation, that the bodies should not remain upon the cross on the Sabbath day, (for that Sabbath day was an high day,) besought Pilate that their legs might be broken, and that they might be taken away. Then came the soldiers, and brake the legs of the first, and of the other which was crucified with him. But when they came to Jesus, and saw that he was dead already, they brake not his legs" (John 19:16, 31-33).

CRUCIFIXION, INCLUDING BREAKING THE LEGS OF THE VICTIMS, WAS PRACTICED IN ANCIENT AMERICA.

"The Mexicans were accustomed to break the legs of a crucified person on one of their most solemn festivals, and to leave him to die upon the cross. This curious fact is stated by Motolinia in the tenth chapter of the first part of his inedited treatise concerning the idolatry of the Indians of New Spain" (Kingsborough. *Antiquities of Mexico,* Vol. 8, p. 16).

3.11. THE CROSS WAS A SACRED SYMBOL OF THE CHRISTIANS.

The most popular symbol of Christianity is the cross. It is found on churches, pulpits, windows, and car bumpers.

"And after that they had mocked him, they took the robe off from him, and put his own raiment on him, and led him away to crucify him" (Matthew 27:31).

"Then Jesus beholding him loved him, and said unto him...come, take up the cross, and follow me" (Mark 10:21).

"And he bearing his cross went forth into a place called the place of a skull, which is called in the Hebrew Golgotha" (John 19:17).

THE CROSS WAS A SACRED SYMBOL OF THE ANCIENT AMERICANS.

Catholicism "... had many similarities of their own to commend them to the natives...the cross, so wide-spread as a symbol, held a high religious significance also here..." (Bancroft. *History of Mexico,* Vol. 2, p. 182).

Hernando Cortez "...was amazed by the sight of a cross, of stone and lime, about ten palms high...it must be regarded as a curious fact, that the Cross should have been venerated as an object of religious worship both in the New World, and in the regions of the Old, where the light of Christianity had never risen" (Prescott. *History of the Conquest of Mexico,* Vol. 1, pp. 254-255; see also p. 273).

Grijalva "... was astonished also at the sight of large stone crosses, evidently objects of worship, which he met with in various places (in Yucatan)" (Prescott. *History of the Conquest of Mexico,* Vol. 1, pp. 219-220).

Burland wrote about the sacred symbol of the white cross upon the holy garments of their priests (Burland, C.A. *The Gods of Mexico,* p. 131).

Glaser wrote about the worship of the cross at Palenque (Glaser. *Indians or Jews?* p. 13).

The Temple of the Foliated Cross in Chiapas Mexico symbolized the god of maize "bread of life" emerging from the earth (the Resurrection?) (National Geographic Society, *National Parks of North America,* p. 315).

Nicholson wrote that the Maya and Christians had many parallels, including the cross symbol (Nicholson. *Mexican and Central American Mythology,* pp. 21, 38, see also pp. 46, 123).

Toor said the Maya cross was their most sacred symbol (Toor. *A Treasury of Mexican Folkways,* pp. 104-106).

3.12. "CARRYING THE CROSS," WAS THE PRACTICE OF THE CHRISTIANS.

"... Whosoever will come after me, let him deny himself, and take up his cross, and follow me" (Mark 8:34; Matthew 10:38; Mark 10:21 and Luke 14:27).

"CARRYING THE CROSS," WAS THE PRACTICE OF THE ANCIENT AMERICANS.

The *Codex Fejervary-Mayer,* a pre-conquest manuscript, shows the bearded god of the Pochtecas carrying a cross (See the Front Cover and page iv of this study).

The Pochtecas were followers of Quetzalcoatl (Nicholson. *Mexican and Central American Mythology, p.* 93).

3.13. "SACRAMENT OF THE LORD'S SUPPER" WAS OBSERVED BY THE CHRISTIANS.

"And as they were eating, Jesus took bread, and blessed it, and brake it, and gave it to the disciples, and said, Take, eat; this is my body. And he took the cup, and gave thanks, and gave it to them, saying Drink ye all of it; For this is my blood of the new testament, which is shed for many for the remission of sins" (Matthew 26:26-28).

"Whoso eateth my flesh, and drinketh my blood, hath eternal life; and I will raise him up at the last day" (John 6:54).

A RITE SIMILAR TO THE SACRAMENT WAS OBSERVED BY SOME ANCIENT AMERICANS:

"Further, the new rites and doctrine (of Catholicism) had many similarities to their own to commend them to the natives...the communion was taken in different forms, as water or bread, and as pieces from the consecrated dough statue of the chief god, the latter form being termed teoqualo, 'god is eaten" (Bancroft. *History of Mexico,* Vol. 2, p. 182). The Aztecs ate pieces of the seed statue of their God (Toor. *A Treasury of Mexican Folkways,* p. 104).

"Aztec priests were seen to prepare a cake of flour, mixed with blood, which they consecrated and gave to the people, who, as they ate, showed signs of humiliation and sorrow, declaring it was flesh of Deity" (Prescott. *History of the Conquest of Mexico,* Vol. 3, p. 314).

3.14. BAPTISM WAS PERFORMED BY CHRISTIANS.

"Go...teach all nations, baptizing them in the name of the Father, the Son, and the Holy Ghost" (Matthew 28:19).

"He that believeth and is baptized shall be saved; but he that believeth not shall be damned" (Mark 16:16).

BAPTISM WAS PERFORMED BY SOME ANCIENT AMERICANS.

"As the natives learned more about Catholicism, they found many beliefs and practices in it that were similar to their own

...both believed in baptism, confession, fasting" (Toor. *A Treasury of Mexican Folkways,* p. 104 and see p. 119).

Peter Martyr noticed the similarities between the rites of the Indians and the Europeans. They both had the sacrament of baptism (Glaser. *Indians or Jews?* p. 14).

Baptisms were performed in a temple of Tenochtitlan (Honore, *In Quest of the White God,* p. 33).

3.15. BAPTISM WAS DESCRIBED AS BEING "BORN OF WATER" ACCORDING TO THE CHRISTIANS.

"Jesus answered, Verily, verily, I say unto thee, Except a man be born of water and of the Spirit, he cannot enter into the kingdom of God" (John 3:5).

BAPTISM WAS DESCRIBED AS BEING "BORN OF WATER" ACCORDING TO SOME ANCIENT AMERICANS.

"On the third, Akbal, he is born of water (the ancient prehistoric peoples had baptismal ceremonies)" (Nicholson. *Mexican and Central American Mythology,* p. 49, see also pp. 110, 116).

3.16. BAPTISM MEANS TO BE "BORN AGAIN" AMONG THE CHRISTIANS.

"Jesus answered and said unto him, Verily, verily, I say unto thee, Except a man be born again, he cannot see the kingdom of God...That which is born of the flesh is flesh; and that which is born of the Spirit is spirit. Marvel not that I said unto thee, Ye must be born again" (John 3:3-7).

BAPTISM MEANS TO BE "BORN ANEW" AMONG THE ANCIENT AMERICANS.

"A ceremony called baptism also existed among the Mayas, the word in their language meaning 'to be born anew'" (Toor. *A Treasury of Mexican Folkways,* p. 119).

3.17. JESUS TAUGHT AS "ONE WHO SPEAKS WITH AUTHORITY."

"And they were astonished at his doctrine: for he taught them as one that had authority, and not as the scribes (Mark 1:22).

THE NAHUA INDIANS OF CENTRAL MEXICO TAUGHT AS "ONE WHO SPEAKS WITH AUTHORITY."

"The very name Nahua...means one who speaks with authority" (Nicholson. *Mexican and Central American Mythology,* p. 15).

3.18. THE PROPHET MELCHIZEDEK WAS KNOWN TO THE CHRISTIANS.

"If therefore perfection were by the Levitical Priesthood, (for under it the people received the law,) what further need was there that another priest should rise after the order of Melehizedek, and not be called after the order of Aaron?" (Hebrew 7:11; see also 5:6; 7:17, 21).

THE PROPHET MELCHIZEDEK WAS KNOWN TO SOME ANCIENT AMERICANS.

"Thus it was recorded <by> the first sage, Melchize <dek>...Written *Merchise* in the Maya text. The presence of an *r* indicates a European word or name, but it does not follow that it was an *r* in Spanish. R and I sounded alike to the Maya ear..." (Roys. *The Book of Chilam Balam of Chumayel, p.*116).

3.19. **TWO CLASSES OF PRIESTHOOD WERE AMONG THE CHRISTIANS.**

"If therefore perfection were by the Levitical priesthood, (for under it the people received the law,) what further need was there that another priest should rise after the order of Melchizedek, and not be called after the order of Aaron? (Hebrews 7:11).

TWO CLASSES OF PRIESTHOOD WERE AMONG SOME ANCIENT AMERICANS.

The Aztecs had a course of study for entrance into the junior priesthood, sometimes called the lowest order of priesthood which the Nacom (war captains) held

(Burland, C.A. *The Gods of Mexico,* p. 70; Nicholson *Mexican and Central American Mythology; p.* 120; Von Hagen, *The Ancient Slun Kingdoms of the Americas,* p. 303).

The highest order of priesthood was for the *Chilam Balam,* the priests or prophets of the Jaguar-god (Makemson. *The Book of the Jaguar Priest,* [*The Book of Chilam Balam of Tizimin*], p. 140).

3.20. **THE OFFICE OF HIGH PRIEST WAS AMONG THE CHRISTIANS.**

"For every high priest taken from among men is ordained for men in things pertaining to God" (Hebrews 5:1).

THE OFFICE OF HIGH PRIEST WAS AMONG SOME ANCIENT AMERICANS.

The High Priest was next in authority to the Emperor among the Aztecs. He supervised the workers of the Temples (Burland, C.A. *The Gods of Mexico,* p. 64).

3.21. **TEMPLE WORSHIP WAS IMPORTANT TO THE CHRISTIANS.**

Jesus cast the moneychangers out of Herod's Temple saying, "It is written, My house shall be called the house of prayer; but ye have made it a den of thieves" (Matthew 21:13).

"And daily in the temple, and in every house, they ceased not to teach and preach Jesus Christ" (Acts 5:42).

TEMPLE WORSHIP WAS IMPORTANT TO SOME ANCIENT AMERICANS.

"The most powerful sacred place in the Aztec empire was Coatepec or Serpent Mountain, the ritual name of the Great Temple of Tenochtitlan...The Aztec temple symbolic mountain stood in the center of the ceremonial precinct of the capital, which was the political center of an empire of more than four hundred towns and fifteen million people" (Carrasco. *Religions of Mesoamerica*, p. 70).

The priests and women dedicated themselves to the temple (Toor. *A Treasury of Mexican Folkways*, p. 104).

3.22.   THE CHRISTIANS HAD POWER TO HEAL THE SICK.

"And when he had called unto him his twelve disciples, he gave them power against unclean spirits, to cast them out, and to heal all manner of sickness and all manner of disease" (Matthew 10:1).

"Is any sick among you? Let him call for the elders of the church; and let them pray over him, anointing him with oil in the name of the Lord: and the prayer of faith shall save the sick..." (James 5:14-15).

SOME ANCIENT AMERICANS HAD POWER TO HEAL THE SICK.

The third (temple) is for healing, Quetzalcoatl's priests were called healers or physicians" (Nicholson. *Mexican and Central American Mythology*, p. 83).

3.23.   SPIRITS HAVE SHAPE, ACCORDING TO THE CHRISTIANS.

"Jesus himself stood in the midst of them...But they were terrified and affrighted, and supposed that they had seen a spirit. And he said unto them...Handle me and see; for a spirit hath not flesh and bones as ye see me have" (Luke 24:36-39).

"Be not forgetful to entertain strangers: for thereby some have entertained angels unawares" (Hebrews 13:2).

SPIRITS HAVE SHAPE, ACCORDING TO SOME ANCIENT AMERICANS.

"In some cases spirits appeared in the natural form of people when they were alive" (Burland and Forman, *The Aztecs, p.* 32).

For more reading about the Indian's beliefs that a man's soul has a human shape (See: Nicholson. *Mexican and Central American Mythology,* p. 42).

3.24.   CHRISTIANS BELIEVED IN HEAVEN.

"I say unto you, that likewise joy shall be in heaven over one sinner that repenteth, more than over ninety and nine just persons, which need no repentance (Luke 15:7).

"For there are three that bear record in heaven, the Father, the Word, and the Holy Ghost: and these three are one" (1 John 5:7).
SOME ANCIENT AMERICANS BELIEVED IN HEAVEN.
"The Mayas believed in immortality and a form of heaven and hell" (Von Hagen. The *Ancient Sun Kingdoms of the Americas,* p. 295, see also p. 116).

3.25. **THE CHRISTIANS TAUGHT THAT THERE WAS A WAR IN HEAVEN.**

"And there was a war in heaven: Michael and his angels fought against the dragon; and the dragon fought and his angels, And prevailed not; neither was their place found any more in heaven. And the great dragon was cast out, that old serpent, called the Devil, and Satan, which deceiveth the whole world: he was cast out into the earth, and his angels were cast out with him" (Revelation 12:7-9).
SOME ANCIENT AMERICANS TAUGHT THAT THERE WAS A WAR IN HEAVEN.
"According to many primary sources the gods were periodically at war with one another during the mythic eras prior to human existence" (Carrasco. *Religions of Mesoamerica,* p. 62).
More reading about the great war in heaven before the creation of the earth (See: Brundage. *The Fifth Sun,* p. 34).

3.26. **CHRISTIANS BELIEVED IN THE RESURRECTION OF THE DEAD.**

"And the graves were opened; and many bodies of the saints which slept arose, And came out of the graves after his resurrection, and went into the holy city, and appeared unto many" (Matthew 27:52-53).
"... there shall be a resurrection of the dead, both of the just and unjust" (Acts 24:15).
"For since by man came death, by man came also the resurrection of the dead" (1 Corinthians 15:21).
SOME ANCIENT AMERICANS BELIEVED IN THE RESURRECTION OF THE DEAD.
"There were a number of parallels between Maya and Christian thought, including the symbolism of the cross and the idea of death and resurrection" (Nicholson. *Mexican and Central American Mythology,* p. 21).

3.27. BETWEEN DEATH AND THE RESURRECTION, MAN GOES TO A SPIRIT WORLD, ACCORDING TO THE CHRISTIANS.

"Verily, verily, I say unto you, The hour is coming, and now is, when the dead shall hear the voice of the Son of God: and they that hear shall live" (John 5:25).

"For Christ...went and preached unto the spirits in prison; Which sometime were disobedient, when once the longsuffering of God waited in the days of Noah, while the ark was a preparing, wherein few, that is, eight souls were saved by water" (1 Peter 3:18-20).

"For this cause was the gospel preached also to them that are dead, that they might be judged according to men in the flesh, but live according to God in the spirit" (1 Peter 4:6).

BETWEEN DEATH AND THE RESURRECTION, MAN GOES TO A SPIRIT WORLD, ACCORDING TO SOME ANCIENT AMERICANS.

"Therefore, the ancients said that when they died, men did not perish, but began to live again almost as if awakened from a dream and that they became spirits or gods" (Carrasco. *Religions of Mesoamerica*, p. 69).

Many Ancient Americans believed that a person's spirit continues to live after death, that it passes from one phase of life to another (Nicholson. *Mexican and Central American Mythology*, p. 42; Toor. *A Treasury of Mexican Folkways*, p. 160; Von Hagen, *The Ancient Sun Kingdoms of the Americas*, pp. 116, 295 and 490).

3.28. CHRISTIANS BELIEVE THAT WHEN INNOCENT CHILDREN DIE, THEY GO TO HEAVEN. NONE ARE CONDEMNED.

"Except ye be converted, and become as little children, ye shall not enter into the kingdom of heaven" (Matthew 18:3).

"But Jesus said, Suffer little children, and forbid them not, to come unto me: for of such is the kingdom of heaven" (Matthew 19:14).

SOME ANCIENT AMERICANS BELIEVE THAT WHEN INNOCENT CHILDREN DIE, THEY GO TO HEAVEN. NONE ARE CONDEMNED.

There is a special paradise in heaven for innocent children and they receive this blessing from God (Nicholson. *Mexican and Central American Mythology*, p. 23; Burland and Forman. *The Aztecs*, pp. 29-30).

3.29. CHRISTIANS BELIEVE THAT THERE ARE THREE HEAVENS.

"There is one glory of the sun, and another glory of the moon, and another glory of the stars: for one star differeth from another star in glory. So also is the resurrection of the dead. It is sown in corruption; it is raised in incorruption" (1 Corinthians 15:41-42).

"I knew a man in Christ...caught up to the third heaven" (2 Corinthians 12:2).

"And if ye call on the Father, who without respect of persons judgeth according to every man's work, passes the time of your sojourning here in fear" (1 Peter 1:17).

SOME ANCIENT AMERICANS BELIEVED THAT THERE ARE THREE HEAVENS.

"They imagined three separate states of existence in the future life. The wicked, comprehending the greater part of mankind, were to expiate their sins in a place of ever-lasting darkness. Another class, with no other merit than that of having died of certain diseases, capriciously selected, were to enjoy a negative existence of indolent contentment. The highest place was reserved, as in most warlike nations, for the heroes who fell in battle, or in sacrifice" (Prescott. *History of the Conquest of Mexico* Vol. 1, p. 82)

(For more information, see: Nicholson. *Mexican and Central American Mythology,* p. 24).

3.30. **IT IS MORE DIFFICULT FOR THE RICH TO ENTER INTO HEAVEN ACCORDING TO CHRISTIANS.**

"Then said Jesus unto his disciples, Verily I say unto you, That a rich man shall hardly enter into the kingdom of heaven. And again I say unto you, It is easier for a camel to go through the eye of a needle, than for a rich man to enter into the kingdom of God" (Matthew 19:23-24).

IT IS MORE DIFFICULT FOR THE RICH TO ENTER INTO HEAVEN ACCORDING TO SOME ANCIENT AMERICANS.

"... our law says that no rich man can enter heaven if a poor man does not lead him by the hand" (Nicholson. *Mexican and Central American Mythology,* p. 68).

3.31. **HELL IS EVERLASTING DARKNESS FOR THE WICKED ACCORDING TO CHRISTIANS.**

"But the children of the kingdom shall be cast out into outer darkness: there shall be weeping and gnashing of teeth" (Matthew 8:12).

"And the angels which kept not their first estate, but left their own habitation, he hath reserved in everlasting chains under darkness unto the judgment of the great day" (Jude 1:6).

HELL IS EVERLASTING DARKNESS FOR THE WICKED ACCORDING TO SOME ANCIENT AMERICANS.

"The wicked, comprehending the greater part of mankind, were to expiate their sins in a place of everlasting darkness" (Prescott. *History of the Conquest of Mexico,* Vol. 1, p. 82).

3.32. THE TRINITY, A THREE-MEMBER GODHEAD, IS WORSHIPPED BY THE CHRISTIANS.

"Go ye therefore, and teach all nations, baptizing them in the name of the Father, and of the Son, and of the Holy Ghost" (Matthew 28:19).

"For there are three that bear record in heaven, the Father, the Word, and the Holy Ghost..." (1 John 5:7).

THE TRINITY, A THREE-MEMBER GODHEAD, IS WORSHIPPED BY SOME ANCIENT AMERICANS:

"Further, the new rites and doctrine (of Catholicism) had many similarities to their own to commend them to the natives. The idea of a trinity was not unknown, and according to the Las Casas's investigations, even a virgin-born member of it" (Bancroft. *History of Mexico,* Vol. 2, p. 182).

"Later divines have found in these teachings of the Toltec god, or high priest, the germs of some of the great mysteries of the Christian faith, as those of the Incarnation, and the Trinity, for example" (Prescott. *History of the Conquest of Mexico,* Vol. 2, p. 5).

"The first is called Caculha Huracan. The second is Chipi Caculha. The third is Raxa-Caculha. And these three are the Heart of Heaven" (Goetz and Morley. *Popol Vuh,* p. 82).

Mayas praised the splendor of the Trinity (Nicholson. *Mexican and Central American Mythology,* pp. 20-21 and 85).

3.33. CHRISTIANS BELIEVED THAT MAN COULD BECOME DIVINE.

"Be ye therefore perfect, even as your Father which is in heaven is perfect" (Matthew 5:48).

"Jesus answered them, Is it not written in your law, I said, Ye are gods?" (John 10:34).

"... we are the children of God: And if children, then heirs; heirs of God, and joint-heirs with Christ..." (Romans 8:16-17).

"Wherefore thou art no more a servant, but a son; and if a son, then an heir of God through Christ" (Galatians 4:7).

"He that overcometh shall inherit all things; and I will be his God, and he shall be my son" (Revelations 21:7).

SOME ANCIENT AMERICANS BELIEVED THAT MAN COULD BECOME DIVINE.

"Therefore, the ancients said that when they died, men did not perish, but began to live again almost as if awakened from a dream and that they became spirits or gods" (Carrasco. *Religions of Mesoamerica,* p. 69).

"For the most part flowers appear to symbolize a fairly high but still intermediate state of the soul on its journey upward to full godhood" (Nicholson. *Mexican and Central American Mythology,* p. 90- 91).

3.34. A BIRD WAS A SYMBOL OF DEITY AMONG THE CHRISTIANS.

"And Jesus, when he was baptized, went up straightway out of the water: and, lo, the heavens were opened unto him, and he saw the Spirit of God descending like a dove, and lighting upon him" (Matthew 3:16).

The dove in the Christian world is the symbol of peace, in remembrance of "the Prince of Peace." It is displayed on churches, in homes, in and on cars, and worn as jewelry by many modern Christians.

A BIRD WAS A SYMBOL OF DEITY AMONG SOME ANCIENT AMERICANS.

"There is luckily no difficulty in translating the name Quetzalcoatl; it means simply Plumed Serpent. The plumes referred to are the exquisite green tail feathers of the once common, now nearly extinct, quetzal (bird) found in Central America" (Brundage. *The Fifth Sun,* p. 102).

"The great bird-serpent, priest-king Quetzalcoatl, is the most powerful figure in all the mythology of Mexico and Central America" (Nicholson. *Mexican and Central American Mythology,* p. 78, see also 110).

The *quetzal,* in commemoration of the sacred bird of the native Americans, is the monetary unit of modern Guatemala, just as the peso is to Mexico and the dollar is to the United States.

3.35. THE SERPENT WAS A SACRED SYMBOL OF SALVATION AMONG THE CHRISTIANS.

"And as Moses lifted up the serpent in the wilderness, even so must the Son of man (Jesus). be lifted up: That whosoever believeth in him should not perish, but have eternal life" (John 3:14-15).

(See the explanation of this book cover on page vii, viii herein).

THE SERPENT WAS A SACRED SYMBOL OF SALVATION AMONG SOME ANCIENT AMERICANS.

The feathered serpent was the symbol of the famous bearded white god who visited ancient America about the time of Christ. His Aztec name was Quetzalcoatl and his Maya name was Kukulcan. Both names mean "feathered serpent" (Burland, C.A. *The Gods of Mexico,* p. 148; Nicholson, *Mexican and Central American Mythology,* p. 78).

3.36. **"LOSE LIFE TO FIND IT" WAS A TEACHING AMONG THE CHRISTIANS.**

"He that findeth his life shall lose it: and he that loseth his life for my sake shall find it" (Matthew 10:39; 16:25 and Mark 8:35).

"LOSE LIFE TO GAIN IT" WAS A TEACHING AMONG SOME ANCIENT AMERICANS.

"The myth was about man, who must learn to glorify god through sensual things, through fine clothes, and music and dance, before he is worthy of breaking the senses one by one and losing his life in order to gain it" (Nicholson. *Mexican and Central American Mythology,* p. 74).

3.37. **THE PARABLE OF THE SOWER WAS TAUGHT BY JESUS CHRIST.**

"...Behold a sower went forth to sow; and when he sowed, some seeds fell by the way side, and the fowls came and devoured them up: Some fell upon stony places, where they had not much earth: and forthwith they sprung up, because they had no deepness of earth: And when the sun was up, they were scorched; and because they had no root, they withered away. And some fell among thorns; and the thorns sprung up, and choked them; But other fell into good ground, and brought forth fruit, some an hundredfold, some sixty-fold, some thirty-fold" (Matthew 13:3-8).

THE PARABLE OF THE SOWER WAS TAUGHT AMONG THE ANCIENT AMERICANS.

In the *Codex Fejervary-Mayer* there is a picture showing remarkable likeness to the Biblical parable of the sower (Nicholson. *Mexican and Central American Mythology* p. 96).

3.38. **COMMUNAL LIVING WAS A WAY OF LIFE AMONG THE CHRISTIANS.**

"And all that believed were together, and had all things common; And sold their possessions and goods, and parted them to all men, as every man had need" (Acts 2:44-45).

"And the multitude of them that believed were of one heart and of one soul: neither said any of them that ought of the things which he possessed was his own; but they had all things common...Neither was there any among them that lacked: for as many as were possessors of lands or houses sold them, and brought the prices of the things that were sold, and laid them down at the apostles' feet: and distribution was made unto every man according as he had need" (Acts 4:32-35).

COMMUNAL LIVING WAS A WAY OF LIFE AMONG SOME ANCIENT AMERICANS.

"Land was communal property: the land was held in common and so between the towns there were no boundaries or landmarks to divide them except when one (city-state) made war on the other" (Von Hagen, *The Ancient Sun Kingdoms of the Americas,* p. 247).

3.39. MARRIAGE CEREMONIES WERE CONDUCTED BY CHRISTIANS.

"And Jesus answering said unto them, The children of this world marry, and are given in marriage" (Luke 20:34).

"Nevertheless, to avoid fornication, let every man have his own wife, and let every woman have her own husband" (1 Corinthians 7:2).

MARRIAGE CEREMONIES WERE CONDUCTED BY THE ANCIENT AMERICANS.

"The rites of marriage were celebrated with as much formality as in any Christian country" (Prescott. *History of the Conquest of Mexico,* Vol. 1, p. 60).

3.40. DIVORCE WAS ALLOWED BY CHRISTIANS.

"It hath been said, Whosoever shall put away his wife, let him give her a writing of divorcement: But I say unto you, That whosoever shall put away his wife, saving for the cause of fornication, causeth her to commit adultery" (Matthew 5:31-32).

DIVORCE WAS ALLOWED BY THE ANCIENT AMERICANS.

"Divorces could not be obtained, until authorized by a sentence of this court, after a patient being of the parties" (Prescott. *History of the Conquest of Mexico,* Vol. 1, p. 61).

3.41. ADULTERY WAS EVIL AMONG CHRISTIANS.

"And Jesus said...out of the heart proceed evil thoughts, murders, adulteries...These are the things which defile a man..." (Matthew 15:16-20).

ADULTERY WAS EVIL AMONG SOME ANCIENT AMERICANS.

"The laws of the Aztecs were registered, and exhibited to the people in their hieroglyphical paintings...Adulterers, as among the Jews, were stoned to death" (Prescott. *History of the Conquest of Mexico,* Vol. 1, p. 59).

To the Aztecs adultery was to be avoided and punished (Burland, C.A. *The Gods of Mexico,* p. 101).

3.42. COMMITTING ADULTERY WITH THE "EYES" WAS SINFUL AMONG CHRISTIANS.

"But I say unto you, That whosoever looketh on a woman to lust after her hath committed adultery with her already in his heart" (Matthew 5:28).

"For from within, out of the heart of men, proceed evil thoughts, adulteries, fornications, murders" (Mark 7:21).

COMMITTING ADULTERY WITH THE "EYES" WAS SINFUL AMONG SOME ANCIENT AMERICANS.

"A more extraordinary coincidence may be traced with Christian rites...But the most striking parallel with (Christian) Scripture is in the remarkable declaration, that 'he who looks too curiously on a woman, commits adultery with his eyes'" (Prescott. *History of the Conquest of Mexico,* Vol. 1, pp. 84, 85).

3.43. RIGHTEOUS LIVING WAS A MAJOR DOCTRINE OF CHRISTIANS.

"Blessed are they which do hunger and thirst after righteousness: for they shall be filled" (Matthew 5:6).

"For the Son of man shall come in the glory of his Father with his angels; and then he shall reward every man according to his works" (Matthew 16:27).

"But in every nation he that feareth him, and worketh righteousness, is accepted with him" (Acts 10:35).

RIGHTEOUS LIVING WAS A MAJOR DOCTRINE OF SOME ANCIENT AMERICANS.

"Quetzalcoatl...taught his people science and morality..." (Honore, *In Quest of the White God* p. 16).

The priests of Quetzalcoatl were educated in schools that taught chastity, prudence, reverence and right living. They were taught to shun filth, vice and anything blameworthy in their lives (Burland, C.A. *The Gods of Mexico,* p. 152).

3.44. CONFESSION WAS PRACTICED BY CHRISTIANS.

"For with the heart man believeth unto righteousness; and with the mouth confession is made unto salvation" (Romans 10:10).

CONFESSION WAS PRACTICED BY SOME ANCIENT AMERICANS.

"Further, the new rites and doctrine (of Catholicism) had many similarities to their own to commend them to the natives...confession was heard by regular confessors, who extended absolution in the name of the deity concerned" (Bancroft. *History of Mexico,* Vol. 2, p. 182).

3.45.   PRAYER WAS PRACTICED BY CHRISTIANS.

"But thou, when thou prayest, enter into thy closet, and when thou hast shut thy door, pray to thy Father which is in secret; and thy Father which seeth in secret shall reward thee openly" (Matthew" 6:6).

PRAYER WAS PRACTICED BY SOME ANCIENT AMERICANS.

"They (the Maya) pray that the eyes of their children may read the writings on the stone tablets" (Makemson. *The Book of the Jaguar Priest [The Book of Chilam Balam of Tizimin]*, p. 5, see also p. 9; Burland, C.A. *The Gods of Mexico*, pp. 152-153; Von Hagen, *The Ancient Sun Kingdoms of the Americas;* pp. 435-436).

3.46.   FASTING, THE ABSENCE OF FOOD AND DRINK FOR SPIRITUAL SUPPORT WAS PRACTICED BY THE CHRISTIANS.

"Moreover when ye fast, be not, as the hypocrites, of a sad countenance: for they disfigure their faces, that they may appear unto men to fast. Verily I say unto you, they have their reward. But thou, when thou fastest, anoint thine head, and wash thy face; That thou appear not unto men to fast, but unto thy Father which is in secret: and thy Father, which seeth in secret, shall reward thee openly" (Matthew 6:16-18).

FASTING, THE ABSENCE OF FOOD AND DRINK FOR SPIRITUAL SUPPORT WAS PRACTICED BY SOME ANCIENT AMERICANS.

"As the natives learned more about Catholicism, they found many beliefs and practices in it that were similar to their own...both believed in baptism, confession, fasting..." (Toor. *A Treasury of Mexican Folkways*, p. 104).

Fasting in ancient America is a topic in other books (Nicholson. *Mexican and Central American Mythology* p. 115; Von Hagen, *The Ancient Sun Kingdoms of the Americas*, pp. 435-436).

3.47.   GREECE HAS INFLUENCED CHRISTIANITY.

The New Testament is known as the "Greek scriptures" because Greek is the most prevalent language of the New Testament manuscripts. Paul, the missionary to the Gentiles, spent most of his ministry in Greece and converted many.

The Christian Church had two kinds of Greek members:

1)   Those of the Jewish lineage who spoke the Greek language. They are referred to in the New Testament as "Hellenists" and "Grecians" (Acts 6:1; 9:29).

2)   Those of the Greek lineage are usually called "Gentiles," and sometimes called "Grecians" in the New Testament (Acts 11:20).

GREECE HAS INFLUENCED SOME ANCIENT AMERICANS.

"The Greek influence persisted in the American Libyan settlements at least until circa A.D.1100 when the tortoise (picture)...was painted by a Mimbres Valley potter in New Mexico. The Libyan language, written alphabetically from left to right or from right to left, and also vertically, was used in New Mexico, as the painting of the American catfish...shows, for the three letters written on the fish spell the Libyo-Egyptian word N-A-R, meaning 'catfish.'" (Fell. *America B.C.*, p. 179).

There are many more parallels between the Greeks and the Ancient Americans (See: Nicholson. *Mexican and Central American Mythology*, p. 16).

3.48. THE ROMAN ROADS USED BY THE EARLY CHRISTIANS WERE SIMILAR TO THE INCA AND MAYA ROADS OF ANCIENT AMERICA.

"There were historically only two road systems: the Roman roads, which covered fifty-six thousand linear miles through Europe, the Near East, and Africa, and that of the Incas, Colombia and along the entire length of desert coast, amounting to more than ten thousand miles of all-weather highways" (Von Hagen. *The Ancient Sun Kingdoms of the Americas*, p. 540 and p. 365).

3.49. WALLED CITIES WERE VERY COMMON IN THE HOLY LAND OF THE CHRISTIANS.

Many near-eastern cities were surrounded by walls, such as Jerusalem (Jeremiah 52:14), Babylon (Jeremiah 51:58), Jericho (Hebrews 11:30), and Tyrus (Ezekiel 26:4).

WALLED CITIES WERE VERY COMMON IN ANCIENT AMERICA.

In the Yucatan there were many walled cities of the ancient Maya. Some of their walls were fifteen feet high, completely surrounding their large towns (Von Hagen. *The Ancient Sun Kingdoms of the Americas*, p. 168, see also p. 219).

3.50. OTHER ROMAN SIMILARITIES WERE FOUND IN ANCIENT AMERICA.

Architecture:

"Just as the use of the arch and a superior, almost imperishable, mortars were the distinguishing characteristics of Roman architecture, lime mortar and the corbeled arch distinguish that of the Maya" (Von Hagen. The *Ancient Sun Kingdoms of the Americas*, p. 312; see also pp. 201, 240).

SHIPS:
"The Romans, who hated the sea and called it 'the pasture of fools,' hugged the coast with their ships. So did the Mayas" (Von Hagen. *The Ancient Sun Kingdoms of the Americas, p.* 375).

3.51. **THE NICKNAME "CHRISTIAN" ORIGINATED FROM FOREIGNERS.**
"Christian. The disciples, we are told (Acts 11:26), were first called Christians at Antioch...It is clear that the appellation 'Christian' was one which could not have been assumed by the Christians themselves...nor could it have come to them from their own nations the Jews; it must, therefore, have been imposed upon them by the Gentile world...it would naturally be used with contempt" (Smith. *Smith's Bible Dictionary,* pp. 106-107).
THE NICKNAME "INDIAN" ORIGINATED FROM FOREIGNERS.
The American "Indians" were so-named by Europeans when the first transatlantic voyages were made from Europe going to the west, thinking that they were on a new route to India. When they arrived in America and encountered a race that was not similar to their own but similar to the race in India, the name was an assumption that their new route was a success, and that they had, in fact, arrived in India; thus, they were named Indians by the Europeans.

3.52. **CHRISTIANS BELIEVED THAT THE FULLNESS OF TRUTH WOULD BE RESTORED TO THE EARTH IN THE LAST DAYS.**
"And he shall send Jesus Christ, which before was preached unto you: Whom the heaven must receive until the times of restitution of all things, which God hath spoken by the mouth of all his holy prophets since the world began" (Acts 3:20-21).
ANCIENT AMERICANS BELIEVED THAT THE FULLNESS OF TRUTH WOULD BE RESTORED TO THE EARTH IN THE LAST DAYS.
"The philosophers and the highest priests knew that the power of Tezcatlipoca would come to an end in the fullness of time, only to be replaced by the more complete worship of Quetzalcoatl" (Burland, C.A. *The Gods of Mexico, p.* 116).

3.53. **CHRISTIANS BELIEVED THAT IN THE LAST DAYS, THE EARTH WILL RETURN TO ITS FIRST STATE OF PARADISE—A NEW EARTH.**
"Nevertheless we, according to his promise, look for new heavens and a new earth, wherein dwelleth righteousness" (2 Peter 3:13).

"And I saw a new heaven and a new earth: for the first heaven and the first earth were passed away; and there was no more sea" (Revelations 21:1).

ANCIENT AMERICANS BELIEVED THAT IN THE LAST DAYS, THE EARTH WILL RETURN TO ITS FIRST STATE OF PARADISE—A NEW EARTH.

"The Mayas envisaged an end when creation would return to its beginnings" (Nicholson. *Mexican and Central Mythology*, p. 20).

YES—CHRISTIANS WERE IN ANCIENT AMERICA!

Section Four

Jesus Christ
Was in
Ancient America

When Hernando Cortez set foot upon the American continent and started to communicate with the Aztecs, it wasn't long before he learned about a popular tradition:

> "...the popular tradition respecting Quetzalcoatl, that deity with fair complexion and flowing beard, so unlike the Indian physiognomy who, after fulfilling his mission of benevolence among the Aztecs, embarked on the Atlantic Sea for the mysterious shores of Tlapallan. He promised on his departure, to return at some future day with his posterity, and resume the possession of his empire" (Prescott. *History of the Conquest of Mexico,* Vol. 1, p. 289).

It was this tradition of a promised return of this white and bearded god that caused the speedy success of the Spanish conquest of Mexico. When the Aztec nation heard that a man of God with a "fair complexion and flowing beard" disembarked from the Atlantic Sea with such miraculous possessions as guns, roaring cannons, horses, huge boats, etc.; and at a time when Quetzalcoatl was most expected, they honored and started to worship Cortez as their returning god.

The Mexican government has commemorated Quetzalcoatl many times with statues, legal documents, stamps, coins, etc. The 1980-1982 five peso coins had his name and leathered serpent symbol on the obverse side. No other person has influenced the ancient and modern history of Mexico as much as Quetzalcoatl. Anciently, he taught them astronomy so advanced it gave Mexico a calendar superior to any other devised by man until the recent atomic age.

And in modern times many thousands of tourists from all over the world flock to the ruins of Mexico each year and hear the tour guides tell of this legendary bearded white god whose symbols are found in visually every ancient ruin site in the Americas.

> "The great bird-serpent, priest-king Quetzalcoatl, is the most powerful figure in all the mythology of Mexico and Central America" (Nicholson. *Mexican and Central American Mythology*, p. 78).

> "If there is any one Aztec god who is known to everyone it is certainly Quetzalcoatl...the only Aztec god human enough for us to idealize" (Brundage. *The Fifth Sun*, p. 102).

Was this Quetzalcoatl a real person or just a fable made up by centuries of legends and traditions?

> "It is beyond dispute that a flesh-and-blood king (Quetzalcoatl) did exist who was a great civilizer and lawgiver, an innovator in arts and crafts, and a man who stood high above his fellows in understanding and rectitude" (Nicholson. *Mexican and Central American Mythology*, p. 79).

WHO WAS QUETZALCOATL?

Quetzalcoatl was a prophet-god who traveled throughout Ancient America, healing and teaching the people. The name "Quetzalcoatl" means "feathered serpent." His name among the Maya was "Kukulcan," which also means "feathered serpent."

Theory #1
Some Say He Was a Man Inspired by Satan.

This is because of the meaning of Quetzalcoatl, which is "feathered serpent." Many believers of the Bible say that the name serpent proves that he is of the devil because Satan was called a serpent in the Garden of Eden story in Genesis Chapter 3.

But, what those believers do not understand is that –in the Bible there are evil serpents and Holy Serpents.

We all know that the serpent in the Garden of Eden was an evil serpent, it was Satan.

But, as identified on pages three and four of this study three holy serpents on the cover of this book are identified as:

1. The Israelite Savior - Moses' Serpent lifted up on a pole.

"And as Moses lifted up the serpent on the wilderness, even so must the *Son of man* be lifted up..." (John 3:14).

2. The Christian Savior - Jesus Christ, the Son of man, lifted up on the cross.
3. The Ancient American Savior - Quetzalcoatl carrying a cross.

Jesus himself said: "Be wise as serpents..." (Matthew 10:16).
Holy Serpents - of course!

Theory #2
Some Say He Was the Apostle Thomas.

"Quetzalcoatl signifies 'feathered serpent,' the last syllable means, likewise, a 'twin,' which furnishes an argument for Dr. Siguenza to identify this god with the apostle Thomas" (Prescott. *History of the Conquest of Mexico,* Vol. 1, p. 81).

The Greek equivalent of the Armenia name "Thomas" is "Didymus," which means "twin."

Many people have speculated on the identity of this prophet-god, each with their evidences and arguments. With so much Christianity half-hidden among the traditions and myths of the early Americans, it is very possible that one of the apostles was doing exactly what he was commissioned to do:

"Go into all the world, and preach the gospel to every creature" (Mark 16:15).

Theory #3
Some Say He Was the Patriarch Noah.

"McCullon carries the Aztec god up to a still more respectable antiquity, by identifying him with the patriarch Noah" (Prescott. *History of the Conquest of Mexico,* Vol. 1, p. 81).

This conclusion is believed by some people because of the many recorded traditions that the Ancient Americans had about the flood which covered the whole earth.

Their traditions talks about the sky collapsing, and the earth people were killed by the universal "water-over-the-earth" catastrophe.

See also the following references:

Bancroft. *History of Mexico,* Vol. II, p. 182.

Brundage. *The Fifth Sun,* pp. 6 and 47.

Guidoni and Magni. *The Andies.* P. 10.7.

Honore. *In Quiest of the White God,* p.33.

Nicholson. *Mexican and Central American Mythology,* p.56.

Prescott. *History of the Conquest of Mexico,* Vol. 1, p. 81.

Toor. *A Treasury of Mexican Folkways,* pp. 457-459.

Von Hagan. *The Ancient Sun Kingdoms of the Americas,* p. 352.

Theory #4
Some Say He Was Jesus Christ.

If Jesus was the redeemer of the whole world, as Christians claim he was, (1 Timothy 4:10; 1 John 2:2; and 4:14) who—with any amount of reason in their minds—can limit their thinking to suppose that he visited and taught only one small segment of human society, in and around Palestine, for only three years?

It is true that Jesus sent his messengers to preach his gospel to every creature, however, he also told his people:

> "I am the good shepherd, and know my sheep, and am known of mine...And other sheep I have, which are not of this fold (flock): them also I must bring, and they shall hear my voice..." (John 10:14-16).

Many Christians believe he was referring to the Gentiles, however, he said those "other sheep" would hear his voice and he made it very clear that:

> "I am not sent but unto the lost sheep of the house of Israel" (Matthew 15:24).

Since Gentiles are not of the house of Israel they would not be eligible to hear his voice. Could it be that the American Indians might be lost Israelites separated from the fold in Palestine, thus; they are *other sheep to hear his voice?* There are many people who believe they are lost Israelites. There are even a few Christian churches that believe this.

In the book, *Indians or Jews?* by Lynn Glaser published in 1973, the printer Roy V. Boswell makes this comment:

> "This is not the first work, nor will it be the last, on this most interesting subject of Jews in America. I was so impressed with the writer's manuscript; I felt I would be derelict in my

duty to scholarship if this significant contribution were not published" (Glaser. *Indians or Jews?* Preface, p. vii).

During New Testament times, the tribes of Israel were scattered abroad (James 1:1), and during that time, there was a well-established civilization in the Americas. So, if the early Americans were part of the Israelites scattered abroad, it is very likely that they would be visited by the Messiah and hear his voice as he promised. The fold in Jerusalem was visited by Christ for forty days after his resurrection (Acts 1:3), so why is it so unbelievable that he might have visited his other sheep in other parts of the world?

If this theory is true, then it would explain why there was so much Christianity in America even before the conquest by Catholicism. It would also explain why Quetzalcoatl has so many things in common with Jesus as this section will show.

Was Jesus Christ and Quetzalcoatl
One and the Same Person?

If they were one and the same person, then, there should be many things they would have in common.

There are more parallels in this section than any other section in this study. There are only a couple parallels between Quetzalcoatl and Thomas, and between Quetzalcoatl and Noah. It is very obvious that Jesus is the one most likely to be Quetzalcoatl, rather than the Apostle Thomas or the Patriarch Noah.

4.1. JESUS CHRIST LIVED IN HEAVEN BEFORE COMING TO EARTH.

"In the beginning was the Word, and the Word (Jesus) was with God..." (John 1:1).

"And no man hath ascended up to heaven, but he that came down from heaven, even the Son of man which is in heaven" (John 3:13).

"What and if ye shall see the Son of man (Jesus) ascend up where he was before?" (John 6:62).

"And now, O Father, glorify thou me with thine own self with the glory which I had with thee before the world was" (John 17:5).

Quetzalcoatl lived in heaven before coming to earth.

"Quetzalcoatl was born in the highest heaven and there given his cultural commission by the Two Gods. Alternatively, he is born to Mixcoatl and the Earth Mother" (Brundage. *The Fifth Sun*, p. 78).

4.2. JESUS CHRIST HAD A FATHER IN HEAVEN.

"Not every one that saith unto me, Lord, Lord, shall enter into the kingdom of heaven; but he that doeth the will of my Father which is in heaven" (Matthew 7:21).

"Whosoever therefore shall confess me before men, him will I confess also before my Father which is in heaven. But whosoever shall deny me before men, him will I also deny before my Father which is in heaven" (Matthew 10:32-33).

See also Matthew 12:50; 16:17 and John 5:18.

QUETZALCOATL HAD A FATHER IN HEAVEN.

The Mexican Zuiven is, "... the name of the uppermost heaven, the abode of the Creator, Hometecutli, the father of Quetzalcoatl, and the place of his first birth as a divinity" (Brinton. *Myths Of The New World*, p. 95).

"A new wisdom shall dawn upon the world universally, in the east, north, west and south. It shall come from the mouth of God the Father...These are fundamentally prophecies of the return of Kukulcan, or Quetzalcoatl, Mexican culture-hero" (Roys. *The Book of Chilam Balam of Chumayel*, p. 164).

There are many traditions about Quetzalcoatl's Father in heaven (Nicholson. *Mexican and Central American Mythology*, pp. 20, 119 and 127).

4.3. JESUS CHRIST WAS THE FIRSTBORN SON OF HIS FATHER IN HEAVEN.

"For whom he did foreknow, he also did predestinate to be conformed to the image of his Son, that he might be the firstborn among many brethren" (Romans 8:29).

"And unto the angel of the church of the Laodiceans write; These things saith the Amen, the faithful and true witness, the beginning of the creation of God" (Revelation 3:14).

QUETZALCOATL WAS THE FIRSTBORN SON OF HIS FATHER IN HEAVEN.

"The history of Quetzalcoatl is also to be found painted in Codex Vindobonensis. In this document we find that the Creator made all things and that among the first creation was a being who was Quetzalcoatl" (Burland, C.A. *The Gods of Mexico*, p. 161).

4.4. JESUS CHRIST WAS CHOSEN TO COME TO EARTH ON A DIVINE MISSION.

"I have glorified thee on the earth: I have finished the work which thou gavest me to do. And now O Father, glorify thou me with thine own self with the glory which I had with thee before the world was" (John 17:4-5).

"But with the precious blood of Christ, as of a lamb without blemish and without spot; Who verily was foreordained before the foundation of the world" (1 Peter 1:19-20).

QUETZALCOATL WAS CHOSEN TO COME TO EARTH ON A DIVINE MISSION.

"Quetzalcoatl had by now become a famous priest and was skilled in many arts. He had been sent down from heaven to reform men and turn them from their impious ways."

(Brundage. The Fifth Sun, p. 114; see also p. 78).

Before the earth was created there was a committee meeting of the gods to choose among themselves one who would bring light to the future earth. They chose Quetzalcoatl to be that light of the world (Nicholson. *Mexican and Central American Mythology,* pp. 72-73, 75).

4.5. **JESUS CHRIST WAS BORN MIRACULOUSLY OF MARY, A VIRGIN MOTHER.**

"And the angel said unto her, fear not, Mary: for...thou shalt conceive in thy womb, and bring forth a son, and shalt call his name JESUS...Then Mary said...How shall this be, seeing I know not a man? And the angel answered and said unto her, The Holy Ghost shall come upon thee, and the power of the Highest shall overshadow thee: therefore also that holy thing which shall be born of thee shall be called the Son of God" (Luke 1:30-35).

QUETZALCOATL WAS BORN MIRACULOUSLY OF COATLICUE, A VIRGIN MOTHER.

That Quetzalcoatl was born of a virgin, is a popular topic among many writers of this bearded white god, including the following:

Bancroft. *History of Mexico,* 2:182;

Brinton. *Myths of the New World,* pp. 172, 214;

Carrasco. *Religions of Mesoamerica,* pp. 44-45;

Honore. *In Quest of the While God,* p. 34;

Nicholson. *Mexican and Central American Mythology,* pp. 87-88;

Von Hagen. *The Ancient Sun Kingdoms of the Americas,* p. 52.

4.6. **JESUS CHRIST HAD A MAN PREACHING REPENTANCE TO PREPARE THE WAY BEFORE HIM.**

"As it is written in the prophets, Behold, I send my messenger before thy face, which shall prepare thy way before thee. The voice of one crying in the wilderness, Prepare ye the way of the Lord, make his paths straight. John did baptize in the wilderness, and preach the baptism of repentance for the remission of sins" (Mark 1:2-4).

QUETZALCOATL HAD A MAN PREACHING REPENTANCE TO PREPARE THE WAY BEFORE HIM.

"The Aztecs have a tradition of a God suffering and crucified named Quetzalcoatl, and of one preceding Him to prepare the way and call them to repentance" (Kingsborough. Vol. 8, p. 3).

4.7.   **JESUS CHRIST TOLD ABOUT HIS FATHER'S HOUSE IN THE HEAVENS.**

"In my Father's house are many mansions: if it were not so, I would have told you. I go to prepare a place for you" (John 14:2).

QUETZALCOATL TOLD ABOUT HIS FATHER'S HOUSE IN THE HEAVENS.

There is a first House in the sky from which the deity ruled (Burland, C.A. *The Gods of Mexico*, p. 150).

4.8.   **JESUS CHRIST HAD A MORTAL MOTHER AND AN IMMORTAL FATHER.**

"Now the birth of Jesus Christ was on this wise: When as his mother Mary was espoused to Joseph, before they came together, she was found with child of the Holy Ghost" (Matthew 1:18).

"And Simon Peter answered and said, Thou art the Christ, the Son of the living God" (Matthew 16:16).

QUETZALCOATL HAD A MORTAL MOTHER AND AN IMMORTAL FATHER.

"Quetzalcoatl was born in the highest heaven and there given his cultural commission by the Two Gods. Alternatively he is born to Mixcoatl and the Earth Mother" (Brundage. *The Fifth Sun,* p. 78).

Quetzalcoatl was spirit and matter fused together by his immortal father and his mortal mother: (Nicholson. *Mexican and Central American Mythology,* p. 85).

4.9.   **JESUS WAS CALLED THE "WORD" OF GOD.**

"In the beginning was the Word, and the Word was with God...And the Word was made flesh, and dwelt among us..." (John 1:1, 14).

"For there are three that bear record in heaven, the Father, the Word, and the Holy Ghost: and these three are one" (1 John 5:7).

QUETZALCOATL WAS CALLED THE "WORD" OF GOD.

"... the Virgin...declared here...'The word shall descend from heaven.' There was rejoicing over his reign..." (Roys. *The Book of Chilam Balam of Chumayel,* p 82).

"All was created by God our Father and by his Word" (Nicholson. *Mexican and Central American Mythology,* p. 49, see also p. 20).

4.10.   JESUS CHRIST WAS THE CREATOR OF THE WORLD.

"He (the Word, Jesus) was in the world, and the world was made by him, and the world knew him not" (John 1:10).

"And to make all men see what is the fellowship of the mystery, which from the beginning of the world hath been hid in God, who created all things by Jesus Christ" (Ephesians 3:9; Hebrews 1:2).

QUETZALCOATL WAS THE CREATOR OF THE WORLD.

"And his priesthood went even further: They sometimes claimed that he (Quetzalcoatl) created the world and all things in it..." (Brundage. *The Fifth Sun*, p. 123, see also p. 178).

Quetzalcoatl as the creator of all things is well known (Guidoni and Magni. *The Andes*, p. 133; Honore, *In Quest of the White God*, p. 16; Toor. *A Treasury of Mexican Folkways*, p. 459).

4.11.   JESUS WAS THE CREATOR OF MORTAL MAN.

"God said, Let us make man in our image" (Genesis 1:26).

"... God...created all things by Jesus Christ" (Ephesians 3:9).

QUETZALCOATL WAS THE CREATOR OF MORTAL MAN.

"Quetzalcoatl is...credited with created men and women and brought into cultivation maize and the maguey..." (Brundage. *The Fifth Sun*, p. 78).

"... Quetzalcoatl created all men...he had created the first human couple and that he continues to create each child as it is born" (Brundage. *The Fifth Sun*, p. 123).

There are many traditions that say that the White God, Quetzalcoatl had created man (Honore. *In Quest of the White God* p. 68; Nicholson. *Mexican and Central American Mythology*, p. 90; Toor. *A Treasury of Mexican Folkways*, p. xxiv).

4.12.   JESUS GIVES TO MEN THE BREATH OF LIFE.

"And the LORD God formed man of the dust of the ground, and breathed into his nostrils the breath of life; and man became a living soul" (Genesis 2:7).

"Then said Jesus to them again, Peace be unto you: as my Father hath sent me, even so send I you. And when he had said this, he breathed on them, and saith unto them, Receive ye the Holy Ghost" (John 20:21-22).

QUETZALCOATL GIVES TO MEN THE BREATH OF LIFE.

The Toltec religion taught that Quetzalcoatl was the god of the wind and the breath of life (Burland and Forman. *The Aztecs*, pp 45, 48-49; Burland, C.A. *The Gods of Mexico*, pp. x, 87, 130, 148, 154, 168 and 177).

4.13. JESUS IS KNOWN BY MANY DESCRIPTIVE NAMES.

"... thou shalt call his name JESUS" (Matthew 1:21).
"... they shall call his name Emmanuel..." (Matthew 1:23).
"... men say that I the Son of man am?" (Matthew 16:13).
"... a Saviour, which is Christ the Lord" (Luke 2:11).
"... the Word was made flesh..." (John 1:14).
"Behold the Lamb of God..." (John 1:29).
"... We have found the Messias...the Christ..." (John 1:41).
"... Christ, the Son of the living God" (John 6:69).
"Jehovah in the Old Testament" (John 8:58).
"... and that Rock was Christ" (1 Corinthians 10:4).
"Saying, I am Alpha and Omega..." (Revelation 1:11).
"These things saith the Amen" (Revelation 3:14).
"the faithful and true witness" (Revelation 3:14).

QUETZALCOATL IS KNOWN BY MANY DESCRIPTIVE NAMES.

Quetzalcoatl (feathered serpent) by the Aztecs.
Bochica (white mantle of light) in Columbia.
Ce Acatl (the Morning Star) in many locations.
Ehecatl (the wind god) in Mexico.
Gucumatz (feathered serpent) in Guatemala.
Hyustus to the Aymara in Peru.
Kukulcan (feathered serpent) by the Maya in Yucatan.
Nanautzin is a pre-mortal name of Quetzalcoatl.
Sume in Brazil.
Viracocha (who came from the sea) in Peru.
Votan in Chiapas, Mexico.
Wakea (the Healer) in the Pacific islands.
Wixepecpcha in Oajaca.

4.14. JESUS WAS GOD ON EARTH.

"Behold, a virgin shall be with child, and shall bring forth a son, and they shall call his name Emmanuel, which being interpreted is, God with us" (Matthew 1:23).

"In the beginning was the Word (Jesus), and the Word was with God, and the Word was God. The same was in the beginning with God" (John 1:1-2).

"For in him dwelleth all the fullness of the Godhead bodily" (Colossians 2:9). **QUETZALCOATL WAS GOD ON EARTH.**
"It was here (Cholula) that the god Quetzalcoatl...made them acquainted with better forms of government, and a more spiritualized religion, in which the only sacrifices were the fruits and flowers of the season" (Prescott. *History of the Conquest of Mexico,* Vol. 2, p. 5; Burland, C.A. *The Gods of Mexico,* pp. 12 and 43; Toor. *A Treasury of Mexican Folkways,* p. xxiv).

4.15. EVEN THOUGH JESUS WAS A GOD, HE WAS ALSO A MORTAL WHO LIVED, SUFFERED, AND DIED ON EARTH.

The New Testament contains the history of the birth, life, suffering, death and resurrection of Jesus Christ.

EVEN THOUGH QUETZALCOATL WAS A GOD, HE WAS ALSO A MORTAL WHO LIVED, SUFFERED, AND DIED ON EARTH.

"Of the great demiurges Quetzalcoatl was the only one who might be considered close to the Aztecs for, though a god, he had a mortal body and had died or slipped away" (Brundage. *The Fifth Sun*, p. 123; Nicholson, *Mexican and Central American Mythology p.* 79; Von Hagen, *The Ancient Sun Kingdoms of the Americas*, pp. 51-52).

4.16. JESUS WAS UPON THE EARTH ABOUT TWO THOUSAND YEARS AGO.

Even most non-Christian nations use the same world calendar as the Christian nations which start with the birth of Christ, it is an accepted and known fact that Christ lived approximately 2000 years ago. All *B.C.* dates refer to "before Christ," and all *A.D.* dates refer to "anno Domini," which is Latin for "in the year of our Lord (Jesus)."

QUETZALCOATL WAS UPON THE EARTH ABOUT TWO THOUSAND YEARS AGO.

"Kukulcan is Mayan for 'Feathered Serpent,' a direct translation of the Nahuatl (Mexican) 'Quetzalcoatl.' This deity of central Mexico dates back to the Pre-classic period, 1500 BC - 300 AD" (Kelly. *Calendar Animals and Deities*, p. 308). "Quetzalcoatl signifies 'feathered serpent,' the last syllable means, likewise, a 'twin,' which furnishes an argument for Dr. Siguenza to identify this god with the apostle Thomas (Didymous)." (Prescott. *History of the Conquest of Mexico*, Vol. 1, p. 81).

The apostle Thomas was a contemporary with Jesus about 2000 years ago.

The following writers testify that Quetzalcoatl was in America about 2000 years ago:

Burland, C.A. *The Gods of Mexico*, pp. 23, 25, and 26; Nicholson, *Mexican and Central American Mythology*, pp. 79 and 83

4.17. JESUS ORIGINATED THE CALENDAR.

Since nearly all modern calendars are counted from the birth of Jesus Christ, sometimes called the "common era" by non-Christian people, we can consider that he, in a technical sense, originated our calendars.

QUETZALCOATL ORIGINATED THE CALENDAR.
"Quetzalcoatl...was the originator of the calendar" (Toor. *A Treasury of Mexican Folkways,* p. xxiv).

4.18. **JESUS WAS GOD, BUT HE WAS NOT SUPREME. A SUPREME GOD RULED OVER HIM.**
"He (Jesus) shall be great, and shall be called the Son of the Highest: and the Lord God shall give unto him the throne of his father David'" (Luke 1:32).
"In the beginning was the Word, and the Word was with " " (Theo = the Supreme God) and the Word was " " (Theos = the subordinate God). And the Word was made flesh, and dwelt among us..." (John 1:1 and 14; Berry. *The Interlinear Greek - English New Testament, p* 240, and *Greek - English Lexicon,* p. 46, " ."").
"... I (Jesus) go unto the father: for my Father is greater than I" (John 14:28; 5:19 and 7:16).
"But I would have you know, that the head of every man is Christ...and the head of Christ is God" (1 Corinthians 11:3).
See also the following New Testament scriptures:
Luke 10:22; John 5:26, 43; 7:16; 14:28
QUETZALCOATL WAS GOD, BUT HE WAS NOT SUPREME. A SUPREME GOD RULED OVER HIM.
"The god Quetzalcoatl was sent by the supreme god to be an earthly king" (Burland and Forman. *The Aztecs,* p. 14).
The Aztec and Maya priests believed in one supreme god, and Quetzalcoatl was sent to them by that god (Burland, C.A. *The Gods of Mexico,* pp. x, 92 and 130; Nicholson. *Mexican and Central American Myth-ology,* pp. 21 and 114; Toor. *A Treasury of Mexican Folkways,* p. 104).

4.19. **JESUS WALKED ON WATER.**
"But the ship was now in the midst of the sea, tossed with waves; for the wind was contrary. And in the fourth watch of the night Jesus went unto them, walking on the sea. And when the disciples saw him walking on the sea, they were troubled, saying, It is a spirit; and they cried out for fear. But straightway Jesus spake unto them, saying, Be of good cheer; it is I; be not afraid" (Matthew 14:24-27).
QUETZALCOATL WALKED ON WATER.
"Other stories tell of Quetzalcoatl walking across the sea, or even marching through it, when the sea would fall and engulf his pursuers" (Burland, C.A. *The Gods of Mexico,* p. 161).

4.20. **JESUS WALKED THROUGH A SEA.**
"Moreover, brethren, I would not that ye should be ignorant, how that all our fathers were under the cloud, and all passed through the

sea; and were all baptized unto Moses in the cloud and in the sea; And did all eat the same spiritual meat; And did all drink the same spiritual drink: for they drank of that spiritual Rock that followed them: and that Rock was Christ" (1 Corinthians 10:1-4).

QUETZALCOATL WALKED THROUGH A SEA.

"Other stories tell of Quetzalcoatl walking across the sea, or even marching through it, when the sea would fall and engulf his pursuers" (Burland, C.A. *The Gods of Mexico, p.* 161).

4.21. JESUS HELPED HIS PEOPLE ENTER THEIR PROMISED LAND.

Referring to the Israelites being let out of Egypt to go to their promised land: "... all our fathers were under the cloud, and all passed through the sea; And were all baptized unto Moses in the cloud and in the sea; And did all eat the same spiritual meat; And did all drink the same spiritual drink: for they drank of that spiritual Rock that followed them: and that Rock was Christ" (1 Corinthians 10:1-4).

QUETZALCOATL HELPED HIS PEOPLE ENTER THEIR PROMISED LAND.

"Thus Quetzalcoatl had to construct a bridge by which his disciples might follow him into the promised land" (Nicholson. *Mexican and Central American Mythology, p.* 91).

4.22. WISDOM FLOWED FROM JESUS.

"And the child (Jesus) grew, and waxed strong in spirit, filled with wisdom: and the grace of God was upon him...And it came to pass, that after three days (when he was twelve years old) they found him in the temple, sitting in the midst of the doctors, both hearing them, and asking them questions. And all that heard him were astonished at his understanding and answers" (Luke 2:40, 46-47).

WISDOM FLOWED FROM QUETZALCOATL.

"From the beginning Quetzalcoatl had been worshiped in Tula...Wisdom flowed from him. Arts, crafts, divination, the study of the sacred calendar" (Brundage. The *Fifth Sun, p.* 115).

4.23. JESUS CHRIST WAS A WHITE MAN.

Publius Lentulus, President of Judea, wrote the following: "There has appeared in our times...a man of great virtue, named Christ Jesus...He is a man of lofty stature, beautiful, having a noble countenance...His face without any spot or wrinkle, but glowing with a delicate flush...He had a beard abundant and the same hazel color as His hair, not long, but forked. His eyes are blue and very bright" (Farrar. *The Life of Christ,* p. 684).

All major paintings of Jesus portray him to be a white man. He was a Jew.

QUETZALCOATL WAS A WHITE MAN.
"The tradition still survives of the god who came as a white man and taught the people the principles of social order, gave them their religion..." (Poindexter. *The Ayar-Incas,* Vol. 1, p. 178).

Quetzalcoatl, "... was said to have been tall in stature, with a white skin, long dark hair, and a flowing beard" (Prescott. *History of the Conquest of Mexico,* Vol. 1, p. 81; pp. 289, 376 and Vol 2, p. 7).

These authors testify that Quetzalcoatl was a white man:

Burland and Forman. *The Aztecs,* pp. 115-116;

Burland. C.A., *The Gods of Mexico,* p. 49;

Herrmann. *Conquest by Man,* p. 168;

Honore. *In Quest of the White God,* [entire book].

4.24. JESUS CHRIST HAD A FULL BEARD.
In the days of Caesar, Lentulus, President of Judea, wrote the following epistle to the Roman Senate: "There has appeared in our times...a man of great virtue, named Christ Jesus... He had a beard abundant and the same hazel color as His hair, not long, but forked" (Farrar. *The Life of Christ,* p. 684).

QUETZALCOATL HAD A FULL BEARD.
"... Quetzalcoatl, that deity with fair complexion and flowing beard, so unlike the Indian..." (Prescott, *History of the Conquest of Mexico,* Vol. 1, p. 289, see also p. 81). "Because he was the only king who ever had a beard, their name for him was 'The Bearded One.'Surely Quetzalcoatl, the Bearded One, was a real person" (Bailey and Grijalva. *Fifteen Famous Latin Americans,* pp. 6, 8). "... he had a long beard—Indians are almost beardless—and he was called Quetzalcoatl after the resplendent *quetzal* bird" (Herrmann. *Conquest by Man,* p. 168).

That Quetzalcoatl had a beard was well known (Burland and Forman. *The Aztecs,* pp. 115-116; Burland. *The Gods of Mexico,* pp.155, 185 and 186; Honore. *In Quest of the White God,* p. 16; Nicholson. *Mexican and Central American Mythology,* p. 82; Toor. *A Treasury of Mexican Folkways,* p.xxv).

4.25. JESUS CHRIST WAS KNOWN AS "GOD OF THE EAST."
"And, behold, the glory of the God of Israel came from the way of the east..." (Ezekiel 43:2).

"When they had heard the king, they departed; and, lo, the star, which they saw in the east, went before them, till it came and stood over where the young child was" (Matthew 2:9).

"For as the lightning cometh out of the east, and shineth even unto the west; so shall also the coming of the Son of man (Jesus) be" (Matthew 24:27).

"And I saw another angel ascending from the east, having the seal of the living God: and he cried with a loud voice to the four angels, to whom it was given to hurt the earth and the sea" (Revelations 7:2). **QUETZALCOATL WAS KNOWN AS "GOD OF THE EAST."**

"Torquemada says the Quetzalcoatl went to 'the lands of Onohualco which are near the sea and are those which today we call Yucatan, Tabasco, and Campeche.' In the *Anales de Chimalpahin*, Quetzalcoatl is called god of the East (Teotl Ixca) of the Nonoualca, which means of the inhabitants of the coast of Tabasco" (Goetz and Morley. *Popol Vuh*, p. 65).

4.26. A BIRD IS A SYMBOL OF JESUS CHRIST.

And Jesus, when he was baptized, went up straightway out of the water: and, lo, the heavens were opened unto him, and he (John) saw the Spirit of God descending like a dove, and lighting upon him (Jesus)" (Matthew 3:16).

This incident caused the dove to be one of the major symbols of Christianity.

A BIRD IS A SYMBOL OF QUETZALCOATL.

"His skin was white and he had a long beard—Indians are almost beardless—and he was called Quetzalcoatl after the resplendent quetzal bird" (Herrmann. *Conquest by Man*, p. 168).

The name "Quetzalcoatl" literally means "bird serpent." The quetzal is a green bird found in Central America (Burland, C.A. *The Gods of Mexico*, p. 148; Nicholson, *Mexican and Central American Mythology*, pp. 78 and 110).

4.27. JESUS CHRIST WAS TEMPTED BY HIS ADVERSARIES.

"Then was Jesus led up of the Spirit into the wilderness to be tempted of the devil" (Matthew 4:1).

QUETZALCOATL WAS TEMPTED BY HIS ADVERSARIES.

"Quetzalcoatl...the fascinating story of his temptation..." (Brundage. *The Fifth Sun*, p. 78).

Other references of Quetzalcoatl's temptations: Burland, C.A. *The Gods of Mexico*, p. 33; Nicholson. *Mexican and Central American Mythology*, pp. 99, 102).

4.28. JESUS CHRIST TAUGHT HIS DISCIPLES TO FAST.

To "fast" is to abstain from food and drink. Prayer and fasting is very common among Christians, for spiritual guidance. "And Jesus said unto them, Can the children of the bride-chamber mourn, as long as the bridegroom is with them? But the days will come, when the bridegroom shall be taken from them, and then shall they fast"

(Matthew 9:15). "Howbeit this kind goeth not out but by prayer and fasting" (Matthew 17:21; Mark 9:29).

QUETZALCOATL TAUGHT HIS DISCIPLES TO FAST.

"He was the one who first taught men to invoke the gods properly, to erect temples, and to institute rituals. Fasting, chastity...were at the core of his teaching..." (Brundage, *The Fifth Sun,* p. 116).

4.29. JESUS CHRIST FASTED FOR FORTY DAYS.

"Then was Jesus led up of the Spirit into the wilderness to be tempted of the devil. And when he had fasted forty days and forty nights, he was afterward an hungered" (Matthew4:1-2).

It is also very interesting that Moses, the Israelite prophet, also fasted for forty days and forty nights:

"When I was gone up into the mount to receive the tables of stone, even the tables of the covenant which the LORD made with you, then I abode in the mount forty days and forty nights, I neither did eat bread nor drink water" (Deuteronomy 9:9).

QUETZALCOATL FASTED FOR FORTY DAYS.

"'...the above mentioned histories all declare that a white man preached among them a holy law, and the fast of forty days.' Having introduced Quetzalcoatl (sic) in his last sentence above, Boturini goes on to compare this culture hero to Christ" (Glaser. *Indians or Jews?* p. 13). Another Aztec King fasted and prayed for forty days (Prescott. *History of the Conquest of Mexico,* Vol. 1, p. 194).

4.30. JESUS CHRIST PREACHED PEACE.

Isaiah prophesied about the birth of Jesus, the *Prince of Peace:*

"For unto us a child is born, unto us a son is given: and the government shall be upon his shoulder: and his name shall be called Wonderful, Counselor, The mighty God, the everlasting Father, The Prince of Peace" (Isaiah 9:6).

"Peace I leave with you, my peace I give unto you: not as the world giveth, give I unto you" (John 14:27).

"The word which God sent unto the children of Israel, preaching peace by Jesus Christ..." (Acts 10:36; Ephesians 2:13-17 and Luke 24:36).

QUETZALCOATL PREACHED PEACE.

"Quetzalcoatl...taught his people science and morality, gave them wise laws, and showed them how to till their land. He forbade human sacrifice and preached peace" (Honore. *In Quest of the White God,* p. 16).

4.31. JESUS CHRIST HEALED THE SICK.

"And Jesus went about all Galilee, teaching in their synagogues, and preaching the gospel of the kingdom, and healing all manner of sickness and all manner of disease among the people" (Matthew 4:23).

QUETZALCOATL HEALED THE SICK.

Quetzalcoatl was known as the Lord of Healing.

(Burland and Forman. *The Aztecs, p.* 43, see also p. 52; Nicholson. *Mexican and Central American Mythology,* p. 127).

4.32.   **JESUS CHRIST TAUGHT HIS DISCIPLES ABOUT CHASTITY.**

"But I say unto you, that whosoever looketh on a woman to lust after her hath committed adultery with her already in his heart" (Matthew 5:28).

"For from within, out of the heart of men, proceed evil thoughts, adulteries, fornications, murders" (Mark 7:21).

QUETZALCOATL TAUGHT HIS DISCIPLES ABOUT CHASTITY.

"He was the one who first taught men to invoke the gods properly, to erect temples, and to institute rituals. Fasting, chastity...were at the core of his teaching..." (Brundage. *The Fifth Sun,* p. 116).

The priests of Quetzalcoatl lived chastely and virtuously (See Nicholson. *Mexican and Central American Mythology,* p. 79).

4.33.   **PERFECTION IS A GOAL FOR MAN ACCORDING TO JESUS CHRIST.**

"Be ye therefore perfect, even as your Father which is in heaven is perfect" (Matthew 5:48).

PERFECTION IS A GOAL FOR MAN ACCORDING TO QUETZALCOATL.

"A series of priests called Quetzalcoatl...were supposed to be perfect in all customs, exercises, and doctrines" (Nicholson. *Mexican and Central American Mythology,* p. 79).

4.34.   **JESUS CHRIST TAUGHT THAT MAN CAN BECOME DIVINE.**

"For a good work we stone thee not; but for blasphemy; and because that thou, being a man, makest thyself God. Jesus answered them, Is it not written in your law, I said, Ye are gods?" (John 10:33-34).

"...we are the children of God: And if children, then heirs; heirs of God, and joint-heirs with Christ; if so be that we suffer with him, that we may be also glorified together"

(Romans 8:16-17).

QUETZALCOATL TAUGHT THAT MAN CAN BECOME DIVINE.

"... The blossoms adorning Quetzalcoatl's headdress are...to symbolize a fairly high but still intermediate state of the soul (of man) on its journey upward to full godhood" (Nicholson. *Mexican and Central American Mythology*, p. 90; see also pp. 49, 52 and 91).

4.35. **THE FAME OF JESUS CHRIST WAS SPREAD ABROAD IN HIS LANDS.**

"And the fame (of Jesus) hereof went abroad into all that land...But they, when they were departed, spread abroad his fame in all that country" (Matthew 9:26, 31).

THE FAME OF QUETZALCOATL WAS SPREAD ABROAD IN HIS LANDS.

"Quetzalcoatl had by now become a famous priest and was skilled in many arts...By this time his fame and holiness were abroad in the land and he was treated as a god...From the beginning Quetzalcoatl had been worshiped in Tula..." (Brundage. *The Fifth Sun*, pp. 114-115).

4.36. **JESUS CHRIST HAD GREAT COMPASSION AND MERCY UNLIKE THE HEATHEN GODS.**

"But when he (Jesus) saw the multitudes, he was moved with compassion on them, because they fainted, and were scattered abroad, as sheep having no shepherd" (Matthew 9:36).

"So Jesus had compassion on them, and touched their eyes: and immediately their eyes received sight, and they followed him" (Matthew 20:34).

QUETZALCOATL HAD GREAT COMPASSION AND MERCY UNLIKE THE HEATHEN GODS.

"... Quetzalcoatl as the creator of all things, and certainly, of all the gods, he most resembled a compassionate being" (Brundage, *The Fifth Sun*, p. 178).

"... the popular tradition respecting Quetzalcoatl, that deity with fair complexion and flowing beard, so unlike the Indian physiognomy who, after fulfilling his mission of benevolence among the Aztecs..." (Prescott. *History of the Conquest of Mexico*, Vol. 1, p. 289).

There is, "... the mistaken idea that the basic religion of middle America was founded on human sacrifice and the tearing out of hearts. The human acts of blood rituals and licensed homicide came later, and were a distortion of what must once have been an extraordinarily complete vision of the place of man and of organic life in the universe...a religion of love and of consciousness became debased into a cult of the master race... (from) a religion whose inner aim was the same as that of all great systems of thought: consciousness, love, and union with the creator of the universe" (Nicholson. *Mexican and Central American Mythology*, pp. 10-11; see also p. 70).

4.37. JESUS CHRIST GAVE DIVINE AUTHORITY AND POWER TO HIS DISCIPLES.

"And when he had called unto him his twelve disciples, he gave them power against unclean spirits, to cast them out, and to heal all manner of sickness mad all manner of disease" (Matthew 10:1).

"Ye have not chosen me, but I have chosen you, and ordained you..." (John 15:16).

QUETZALCOATL GAVE DIVINE AUTHORITY AND POWER TO HIS DISCIPLES.

"He (Seler) believes that what he calls 'royal rank' among the Mexicans went back in the first instance to Quetzalcoatl and the Toltec dynasty, and we have already seen how Landa traces the authority of the 'lords' of Yucatan back to the same source" (Roys. *The Book of Chilam Balam of Chumayel,* p. 198).

4.38. THE DISCIPLES OF JESUS CHRIST WERE GIVEN AUTHORITY TO HEAL PEOPLE.

"After these things the Lord appointed other seventy also, and sent them two and two...And into whatsoever city ye enter, and they receive you, eat such things as are set before you and heal the sick that are therein...And the seventy returned again with joy, saying, Lord, even the devils are subject unto us through thy name" (Luke 10:1-17).

"Is any sick among you? Let him call for the elders of the church; and let them pray over him, anointing him with oil in the name of the Lord: and the prayer of faith shall save the sick..." (James 5:14-15).

THE DISCIPLES OF QUETZALCOATL WERE GIVEN AUTHORITY TO HEAL PEOPLE.

"Quetzalcoatl's priests being called healers..." (Nicholson. *Mexican and Central American Mythology,* p. 83).

Some healers of Quetzalcoatl used an image of him to heal the patient (Burland and Forman. *The Aztec,* p. 52).

4.39. THE PARABLE OF THE SOWER WAS TAUGHT BY JESUS CHRIST.

"Behold a sower went forth to sow; And...some seeds fell by the way side, and the fowls...devoured them up: Some fell upon stony places, where they had not much earth...And some fell among thorns; and the thorns sprung up, and choked them:

But other fell into good ground, and brought forth fruit..." (Matthew 13:3-8).

The interpretation:

"When any one heareth the word of the kingdom, and understandeth it not, then cometh the wicked one, and catcheth away that which was sown in the heart. This is he which received seed by the way side. But he that received the seed into stony places, the same is he that heareth the word, and anon with joy receiveth it; Yet hath he not root in himself, but...when tribulation or persecution ariseth...he is offended. He also that received seed among the thorns is he that heareth the word; and the care of this world, and...of riches, choke the word, and he becometh unfruitful. But he that received seed into the good ground is he that heareth the word, and understandeth it; which also beareth fruit..." (Matthew 13:19-23).

THE PARABLE OF THE SOWER WAS TAUGHT BY QUETZALCOATL.

"...in the *Codex Fejervary-Mayer* there is a fourfold picture showing the varying fortunes of a maize plant and bearing a remarkable likeness to the Biblical parable of the sower" (Nicholson. Mex. *and Central Amer. Mythology*, p. 96).

4.40.   JESUS CHRIST WAS THE HEAD OF THE TRUE CHURCH IN THE NEW TESTAMENT.

"...upon this rock I will build my church; and the gates of hell shall not prevail against it" (Matthew 16:18).

"The beginning of the gospel of Jesus Christ, the Son of God" (Mark 1:1).

"For the husband is the head of the wife, even as Christ is the head of the church: and he is the savior of the body" (Ephesians 5:23; 1:22).

QUETZALCOATL WAS THE HEAD OF THE TRUE CHURCH IN ANCIENT AMERICA.

"The tradition still survives of the god (Quetzalcoatl) who came as a white man and taught the people the principles of social order, gave them their religion..." (Poindexter. *The Ayar Incas,* Vol. 1, p. 178).

"He (Quetzalcoatl) made them acquainted with...a more spiritualized religion, in which the only sacrifices were the fruits and flowers of the season" (Prescott. *History of the Conquest of Mexico,* Vol. 2, p. 5).

Quetzalcoatl originated America's religion of mercy (Burland and Forman, *The Aztecs,* p. 43; Burland, C.A. *The Gods of Mexico,* p. 66; Nicholson. *Mexican and Central American Mythology,* pp. 79 and 91; Toor. *A Treasury of Mexican Folkways,* p. xxiv).

4.41.   THE "FIRST DAY" WAS REVERED AS THE LORD'S DAY, THE DAY OF JESUS CHRIST.

"... the first day of the week, came Mary Magdalene and the other Mary to see the sepulchre. And...the angel of the Lord descended...and said unto the women...He is not here: for he is risen..." (Matthew 28:1-6).

"And upon the first day of the week, when the disciples came together to break bread..." (Acts 20:7).

"Upon the first day of the week let every one of you lay by him in store, as God hath prospered him, that there be no gatherings when I come" (1 Corinthians 16:2).

THE "FIRST DAY" WAS REVERED AS THE DAY OF QUETZALCOATL.

"Another name for Quetzalcoatl was Ce Acatl, One Reed...They named this period Ce Acatl after its first day, One Reed, which they said was the sign of Quetzalcoatl" (Burland, C.A. *The Gods of Mexico*, p. 150).

4.42. JESUS CHRIST WAS "GOD OF THE WIND."

"Then he (Jesus) arose, and rebuked the winds and the sea; and there was a great calm. But the men marveled, saying, What manner of man is this, that even the winds and the sea obey him!" (Matthew 8:26-27; see also Mark 4:39-41 and Luke 8:25).

QUETZALCOATL WAS "GOD OF THE WIND."

"Among the gods of Teotihuacan the rain spirit, Tlaloc, was most important, but the feathered Serpent (Quetzalcoatl), in his guise as a wind god, was prominent..." (Burland and Forman. *The Aztecs*, pp. 13-14, 46 and 49).

Quetzalcoatl was god of the wind and the breath (Burland, C.A. *The Gods of Mexico*, pp. x; 21 and 87; Yoor, *A Treasury of Mexican Folkways*, p. 458).

4.43. JESUS CHRIST WAS THE SAVIOR OF THE WORLD.

"For unto you is born this day in the city of David a Saviour, which is Christ the Lord" (Luke 2:11).

"... Now we believe, not because of thy saying: for we have heard him ourselves, and know that this is indeed the Christ, the Saviour of the world" (John 4:42).

QUETZALCOATL WAS THE SAVIOR OF THE WORLD.

The Aztecs prayed to Quetzalcoatl, the Savior of all mankind (Burland, C.A. *The Gods of Mexico*, pp. 152-153; Nicholson, *Mexican and Central American Mythology*, p. 109).

4.44. JESUS CHRIST SENT MISSIONARIES OUT TO PREACH AND BRING CONVERTS INTO THEIR RELIGION.

"... The Lord appointed other seventy also, and sent them two and two before his face into every city and place, whither he himself would come..." (Luke 10:1-3).

"Go ye therefore, and teach all nations, baptizing them in the name of the Father, and of the Son, and of the Holy Ghost: Teaching them to observe all things whatsoever I have commanded you..." (Matthew 28:19-20).

QUETZALCOATL SENT MISSIONARIES OUT TO PREACH AND BRING CONVERTS INTO THEIR RELIGION.

"That the new religion (of Quetzalcoatl) was a proselytizing one we gather from the fact that the servitors of the god under the high priest were said to be noted travelers, going to far places and preaching from hilltops...To achieve his ends he formed a special group of priests with voices like trumpets, who called the people to penance and the new light" (Brundage. *The Fifth Sun*, pp. 113-115).

4.45. **JESUS CHRIST WAS THE "KING" OF THE EARTH.**

"And when he (Jesus) was come nigh, even now at the descent of the mount of Olives, the whole multitude of the disciples began to rejoice and praise God with a loud voice for all the mighty works that they had seen; Saying, Blessed be the King that cometh in the name of the Lord: peace in heaven, and glory in the highest" (Luke 19:37-38).

"And they began to accuse him, saying, We found this fellow perverting the nation, and forbidding to give tribute to Caesar, saying that he himself is Christ a King" (Luke 23:2).

QUETZALCOATL WAS THE "KING" OF THE EARTH.

"According to one tradition the Mexican throne had belonged to Quetzalcoatl himself, who had been its legendary first incumbent" (Brundage. *The Fifth Sun*, p. 125).

"With the Toltecs we enter recorded history, though it begins with the myth of the god Quetzalcoatl, who was sent by the supreme god to be an earthly king" (Burland and Forman. *The Aztecs*, p. 14).

Quetzalcoatl is called a "god-king" and a "priest-king" (Burland, C.A. *The Gods of Mexico*, p. 12; Honore. *In Quest of the White God*, p. 98; Nicholson. *Mexican and Central American Mythology*, pp. 24 and 91).

4.46. **JESUS CHRIST WEPT.**

"And when he (Jesus) had come near, he beheld the city (Jerusalem), and wept over it" (Luke 19:41).

"...Lord, if thou hadst been here, my brother had not died. When Jesus therefore saw her weeping, and the Jews also weeping which came with her, he groaned in the spirit, and was troubled, And said, Where have ye laid him? They said unto him, Lord come and see. Jesus wept. Then said the Jews, Behold how he loved him!" (John 11:32-36).

John 11:35 "Jesus wept" is the shortest verse in the Bible.

QUETZALCOATL WEPT.

Inca Indians of Peru depicted their white god on pottery and cloth as a *weeping god* with lots of tears (Von Hagen. *The Ancient Sun Kingdoms of the Americas*, pp. 416 and 576).

4.47. JESUS CHRIST TAUGHT THAT WHEN PEOPLE DIE, THEIR SPIRITS LIVE IN A SPIRIT WORLD.

"Verily, Verily I say unto you, The hour is coming, and now is, when the dead shall hear the voice of the Son of God: and they that hear shall live" (John 5:25).

"For Christ...being put to death in the flesh, but quickened by the Spirit: By which also he went and preached unto the spirits in prison: Which sometime were disobedient, when once the longsuffering of God waited in the days of Noah, while the ark was a preparing, wherein few, that is, eight souls were saved by water" (1 Peter 3:18-19).

"For this cause was the gospel preached also to them that are dead, that they might be judged according to men in the flesh, but live according to God in the spirit" (1 Peter 4:6).

QUETZALCOATL TAUGHT THAT WHEN PEOPLE DIE, THEIR SPIRITS LIVE IN A SPIRIT WORLD.

"The most important of the ancient (American) beliefs still existing everywhere is that the personality continues after death in much the same way as before" (Toor. *A Treasury of Mexican Folkways*, p. 160).

4.48. "LORD" WAS A TITLE OF JESUS CHRIST.

"And they entered in, and found not the body of the Lord Jesus" (Luke 24:3).

"Wherefore of these men which have companied with us all the time that the Lord Jesus went in and out among us" (Acts 1:21).

"Lord Jesus" is found nearly 200 times in the New Testament.

"LORD" WAS A TITLE OF QUETZALCOATL.

"Only Quetzalcohuatl (sic) among all the gods was preeminently called Lord; in such sort, that when any one swore, saying, By our Lord, he meant Quetzalcohuatl (sic) and no other; though there were many other highly esteemed gods" (Bancroft. *The Native Races of the Pacific States*, Vol, 3, p. 351; Burland, C.A. *The Gods of Mexico*, pp. 152-153).

He is the Lord of Healing (Burland and Forman. *The Aztecs*, 43 and 52).

He is the Lord of Hope (Burland and Forman. *The Aztecs;* pp. 43 and 52).

He is the Lord of the Winds (Burland and Forman, *The Aztecs,* pp. 45, 46, 49; Burland, C.A. *The Gods of Mexico*, p. 150; Burland and Forman. *The Aztecs*, p. 45).

4.49. "LORD OF LIFE" WAS A TITLE OF JESUS.

"Jesus said unto her, I am the resurrection, and the life..." (John 11:25).

Jesus gives life (John 1:4; 6:33; 10:28; 14:6; Colossians 3:4 and 1 John 5:12).

"LORD OF LIFE" WAS QUETZALCOATL.

"The god Quetzalcoatl was also the Lord of Life, who brought penitence, love, and exemption from the usual rituals..." (Burland and Forman. *The Aztecs,* p. 45).

4.50. **JESUS CHRIST WAS KNOWN AS THE "SUN" OR "THE LIGHT OF THE WORLD."**

"But unto you that fear my name shall the Sun of righteousness arise with healing in his wings" (Malachi 4:2).

"Then spake Jesus again unto them, saying, I am the light of the world; he that followeth me shall not walk in darkness, but shall have the light of life" (John 8:12; see also 9:5).

QUETZALCOATL WAS KNOWN AS THE "SUN," OR "THE LIGHT OF THE WORLD."

"Quetzalcoatl was called Lord of the Dawn" (Carrasco. *Religions of Mesoamerica,* pp. 64-65).

Quetzalcoatl is the Sun and also the planet Venus which is swallowed up by the sun (Nicholson. *Mexican and Central American Mythology,* pp. 87 and 91).

4.51. **JESUS CHRIST GIVES TO ALL PEOPLE A CONSCIENCE, OR LIGHT AND KNOWLEDGE TO KNOW GOOD FROM EVIL.**

"In him was life; and the life was the light of men" (John 1:4).

"Jesus" was the true Light, which lighteth every man that cometh into the world" (John 1:10; see 1:4 and 8:12).

QUETZALCOATL GIVES TO ALL PEOPLE A CONSCIENCE, OR LIGHT AND KNOWLEDGE TO KNOW GOOD FROM EVIL.

"... Quetzalcoatl in his capacity as the god of the wind. The wind was also seen as the breath of life, and the wayward flow of intelligence passing through the human mind" (Burland, C.A. *The Gods of Mexico,* p. 87).

The gods told Nanautzin, a manifestation of Quetzalcoatl: Be thou the light of the world. He replied: I accept your order (Nicholson. *Mexican and Central American Mythology,* pp. 73 and 75).

4.52. **"MESSIAH" IS A NAME TITLE OF JESUS CHRIST.**

"He first findeth his own brother Simon, and saith unto him, We have found the Messias, which is, being interpreted, the Christ" (John 1:41; see also Matthew 16:16).

The Greek name title "Christ" is identical to the Hebrew name title "Messiah."

"MESSIAH" IS A NAME TITLE OF QUETZALCOATL.
"Further, the new rites and doctrine (of Catholicism) had many similarities to their own to commend them to the natives...while the mysterious Quetzalcoatl lived in the hopes, especially of the oppressed, as the expected Messiah" (Bancroft. *History of Mexico*, Vol. 2, p. 182).

4.53. A SERPENT IS A SYMBOL OF JESUS CHRIST.
"And as Moses lifted up the serpent in the wilderness, even so must the Son of man (Jesus) be lifted up: that whosoever believeth in him should not perish, but have eternal life" (John 3:14-15).
Jesus, being lifted up on the cross, was a parallel of the serpent being lifted up on the pole by Moses.
A SERPENT IS A SYMBOL OF QUETZALCOATL.
The name Quetzalcoatl means feathered serpent, or plumed serpent, or bird serpent (Burland and Forman. *The Aztecs*, p. 45; Carrasco. *Religions of Mesoamerica*, pp. 44-45; Burland, C.A. *The Gods of Mexico*, p. 34).
A symbol of Quetzalcoatl is an image of a serpent's head with feathers protruding from around the neck.

4.54. JESUS CHRIST WAS KNOWN AS THE GOD OF THE BREAD OF LIFE.
"And Jesus said unto them, I am the bread of life: he that cometh to me shall never hunger; and he that believeth on me shall never thirst" (John 6:35).
QUETZALCOATL WAS KNOWN AS THE GOD OF THE BREAD OF LIFE.
"At Palenque National Park, in the state of Chiapas Mexico there is the Temple of the Foliated Cross, and there inside, a carved panel features a cross symbolizing the god of maize (Quetzalcoatl)—the staff of life—emerging from the earth" (National Geographic Society, *National Parks of North America*, p. 315).
Quetzalcoatl gave human kind the special food, maize (Nicholson. *Mexican and Central American Mythology* p. 90).

4.55. JESUS CHRIST WAS A SHEPHERD, AND A SHEPHERD'S STAFF, OR CROOK WAS ANOTHER OF HIS SYMBOLS.
"I am the good shepherd, and know my sheep, and am known of mine. As the father knoweth me, even so know I the Father: and I lay down my life for the sheep. And other sheep I have, which are not of this fold: them also I must bring, and they shall hear my voice; and there shall be one fold, and one shepherd" (John 10:14-16).

QUETZALCOATL WAS A SHEPHERD, AND A SHEPHERD'S STAFF, OR CROOK WAS ANOTHER OF HIS SYMBOLS.

Another symbol of Quetzalcoatl was the shepherd's staff, which is represented in the night sky as the crook in Leo, the heavenly symbol of this deity (Burland, C.A. *The Gods of Mexico,* p. 94).

4.56. JESUS CHRIST COMMANDED MEN TO LOVE ONE ANOTHER.

"A new commandment I give unto you, that ye love one another; as I have loved you that ye also love one another. By this shall all men know that ye are my disciples, if ye have love one to another" (John 13:34-35).

QUETZALCOATL COMMANDED MEN TO LOVE ONE ANOTHER.

"Tiki viracocha (Peruvian name for Quetzalcoatl), "...was creator of all things and commanded men to be good to one another and live without violence" (Honore. *In Quest of the White God,* p. 16).

4.57. JESUS SET THE EXAMPLE OF HOW WE SHOULD LIVE.

"Jesus saith unto him, I am the way, the truth, and the life: no man cometh unto the Father, but by me" (John 14:6).

"For even hereunto were ye called: because Christ also suffered tier us, leaving us an example, that ye should follow his steps" (1 Peter 2:21).

QUETZALCOATL SET THE EXAMPLE OF HOW WE SHOULD LIVE.

One can "... hope to follow the example of Quetzalcoatl and can reach the Pole of the universe, the heart of all things" (Burland, C.A. *The Gods of Mexico,* p. 94).

4.58. THE KINGDOM OF JESUS CHRIST WAS NOT OF THIS WORLD.

"Jesus answered, My kingdom is not of this world: if my kingdom were of this world, then would my servants fight, that I should not be delivered to the Jews: but now is my kingdom not from hence" (John 18:36).

THE KINGDOM OF QUETZALCOATL WAS NOT OF THIS WORLD.

"Quetzalcoatl's kingdom was not of this world" (Nicholson. *Mexican and Central American Mythology,* p. 93).

4.59. CHRISTIANS TOOK UPON THEMSELVES THE NAME OF CHRIST.

"Jesus" is the most popular given name in Latin countries. "... And the disciples (of Jesus) were called Christians first in Antioch" (Acts 11:26).

ANCIENT AMERICANS TOOK UPON THEMSELVES THE NAME OF QUETZALCOATL.

"When Topiltzin ascended the Toltec throne, he changed his own name to Quetzalcoatl" (Leonard. *Ancient America,* p. 59).

The priesthood leaders of the Toltecs and Aztecs took upon themselves the name of Quetzalcoatl (Burland, C.A. *The Gods of Mexico,* pp. 43 and 154; Nicholson, *Mexican and Central American Mythology,* p. 79).

4.60. JESUS IS A TWIN WITH MOSES.

"The LORD thy God will raise up unto thee a Prophet...like unto me (Moses)...I will raise them up a Prophet like unto thee (Moses)..." (Deuteronomy 18:15, 18).

"This (Jesus) is that Moses, which said unto the children of Israel. A prophet shall the Lord your God raise up unto you of your brethren, like unto me..." (Acts 7:37).

QUETZALCOATL IS A TWIN WITH XOLOTL.

"Quetzalcoatl signifies *feathered serpent.* The last syllable means, likewise, a *twin* which furnished an argument for Dr. Siguenza to identify this god with the apostle Thomas, (Didymus signifying also a twin) who, he supposes, came over to America to preach the gospel" (Prescott. *History of the Conquest of Mexico,* Vol. 1, p. 81).

Since the last syllable of Quetzalcoatl means twin, there are many versions of who the twins are. Some say they are the Morning Star and the Evening Star which represent Quetzalcoatl and Xolotl (Brundage. *The Fifth Sun,* p. 120; Burland and Forman. *The Aztecs,* p. 45; Burland, C.A. *The Gods of Mexico,* p. 102; Nicholson. *Mexican and Central American Mythology,* p. 83).

4.61. JESUS CHRIST WAS A MEDIATOR BETWEEN MEN AND GOD.

"For there is one God, and one mediator between God and men, the man Christ Jesus" (1 Timothy 2:5).

QUETZALCOATL WAS A MEDIATOR BETWEEN MEN AND GOD.

"Quetzalcoatl was important in that he was regarded as the first priest, the founder of the whole priestly order; the human who made the contact not of his own volition but by the will of the gods, between mankind and the supernatural world" (Burland, C.A. *The Gods of Mexico,* p. 66).

4.62. JESUS CHRIST ESTABLISHED THE PRIESTHOOD AMONG HIS FOLLOWERS.

"But this man (Jesus), because he continueth ever, hath an unchangeable priesthood" (Hebrews 7:24).

"Ye also, as lively stones, are built up a spiritual house, an holy priesthood, to offer up spiritual sacrifices, acceptable to God by Jesus Christ" (1 Peter 2:5).

QUETZALCOATL ESTABLISHED THE PRIESTHOOD AMONG HIS FOLLOWERS.

"Quetzalcoatl was important in that he was regarded as the first priest, the founder of the whole priestly order" (Burland, C.A. *The Gods of Mexico,* p. 66, see also p. 93).

4.63. JESUS CHRIST WAS A HIGH PRIEST.

"Whither the forerunner is for us entered, even Jesus, made an high priest for ever after the order of Melchisedec" (Hebrews 6:20).

"But Christ being come an high priest of good things to come..." (Hebrews 9:11).

QUETZALCOATL WAS A HIGH PRIEST.

"Later divines have found in these teachings of the Toltec god (Quetzalcoatl), or high priest, the gems of some of the great mysteries of the Christian faith" (Prescott. *History of the Conquest of Mexico,* Vol. 2, p. 5).

Quetzalcoatl was the great bird-serpent, priest-king who originated the priestly ritual (Burland, C.A. *The Gods of Mexico,* pp. 44 and 95; Nicholson. *Mexican and Central American Mythology,* p. 78; Toor. *A Treasury of Mexican Folkways,* p. xxiv).

4.64. THE MORNING STAR, VENUS, IS A SYMBOL OF JESUS CHRIST.

"Where is he that is born King of the Jews? for we have seen his star in the east, and are come to worship him...the star, which they saw in the east, went before them, till it came and stood over where the young child was" (Matthew 2:2, 9).

"I Jesus am the...root and the offspring of David, and the bright and morning star (Revelation 22:16; Numbers 24:17 and Revelation 2:26-28).

THE MORNING STAR, VENUS, IS A SYMBOL OF QUETZALCOATL.

It was a well known tradition among many people in ancient America that Venus, the morning star, is a symbol of Quetzalcoatl (Burland, C.A. *The Gods of Mexico,* pp. x, 35, 148; Nicholson. *Mexican and Central American Mythology,* p. 83; Roys. *The Book of Chilam Balam of Chumayel,* p. 161; Toor. *Mexican Folkways,* p. xxiv).

4.65. **A SACRAMENT OF THE "LORD'S SUPPER" WAS COMMEMORATED TO REMEMBER JESUS CHRIST.**

"And as they were eating, Jesus took bread, and blessed it, and brake it, and gave it to the disciples, and said, Take, eat; this is my body. And he took the cup, and gave thanks, and gave it to them, saying, Drink ye all of it; For this is my blood of the new testament, which is shed for the remission of sins" (Matthew 26:26-28; see also 1 Corinthians 10:16 and 11:26-27).

A SACRAMENT OF THE "LORD'S SUPPER" WAS COMMEMORATED TO REMEMBER QUETZALCOATL.

"... the communion (among the followers of Quetzalcoatl) was taken in different forms, as wafer or bread, and as pieces from the consecrated dough statue of the chief god, the latter form being termed *teoqualo, god is eaten*" (Bancroft. *History of Mexico,* Vol. 2, p. 182).

The Aztecs had a ceremony to forgive sins by eating small pieces of bread distributed among the faithful. Sometimes the pieces came from a bread statue of their god (Honore. *In Quest of the White God,* p. 34; Toor. *A Treasury of Mexican Folkways,* p. 104).

4.66. **THORNS DREW BLOOD FROM JESUS CHRIST.**

"And the soldiers platted a crown of thorns, and put it on his head, and they put on him a purple robe. And said, Hail, King of the Jews! And they smote him with their hands" (John 19:2; Matthew 27:28-29; Mark 15:17-18).

THORNS DREW BLOOD FROM QUETZALCOATL.

"One text tells that in the year Two Reed, Ce Acatl Quetzalcoatl (another name for the hero) built a special temple facing the cardinal directions...He also set thorns into his flesh on the summit of four sacred mountains near Tollan" (Carrasco. *Religions of Mesoamerica,* p. 61).

Quetzalcoatl stained thorns red with his blood (Brundage. The Fifth Sun, p. 249; Burland, C.A. *The Gods of Mexico,* p. 156; Nicholson. *Mexican and Central American Mythology* p. 73).

4.67. **JESUS CHRIST BELIEVED IN SELF-SACRIFICE.**

"He that findeth his life shall lose it: and he that loseth his life for my sake shall find it" (Matthew 10:39).

"As the Father knoweth me, even so know I the Father: and I lay down my life for the sheep" (John 10:15; 6:51).

"I beseech you therefore, brethren, by the mercies of God, that ye present your bodies a living sacrifice, holy, acceptable unto God, which is your reasonable service" (Romans 12:1).

QUETZALCOATL BELIEVED IN SELF-SACRIFICE.

"The new high priest (messenger of Quetzalcoatl) insisted that his god wanted only the mildest sacrifices, such as flowers and birds, and that he abhorred the effusion of human blood except in auto sacrifice" (Brundage. *The Fifth Sun*, p. 114).

Quetzalcoatl is the god of self-sacrifice (Burland, C.A. *The Gods of Mexico,* p. x).

4.68.   JESUS CHRIST TAUGHT AGAINST HUMAN SACRIFICE.
"Thou shalt not kill" (Exodus 20:13).

"... He that killeth with the sword must be killed with the sword..." (Revelation 13:10).

QUETZALCOATL   TAUGHT   AGAINST   HUMAN SACRIFICE.

"The new high priest (messenger of Quetzalcoatl) insisted that his god wanted only the mildest sacrifices, such as flowers and birds, and that he abhorred the effusion of human blood except in auto sacrifice" (Brundage. *The Fifth Sun*, p. 114; see also p. 208).

That Quetzalcoatl forbade human sacrifice was well known (Carrasco. *Religions of Mesoamerica,* pp. 45 and 62; Burland and Forman. *The Aztecs,* p. 71; Honore. *In Quest of the White God,* p. 16; Nicholson. *Mexican and Central American Mythology,* pp. 10-11, 70).

4.69.   JESUS CHRIST FREELY GAVE HIS LIFE.
"Even as the Son of man (Jesus) came not to be ministered unto, but to minister, and to give his life a ransom for many" (Matthew 20:28).

"As the Father knoweth me, even so know I the father: and I lay down my life for the sheep" (John 10:15).

QUETZALCOATL FREELY GAVE HIS LIFE.

"Quetzalcoatl...was able to reject or accept death just as he wished" (Burland, C.A. The Gods of Mexico, p. 130; Burland and Forman, *The Aztecs,* p. 46).

4.70.   THE BLOOD OF JESUS CHRIST WAS VERY IMPORTANT TO HIS PEOPLE.
"For this is my blood of the new testament, which is shed for many for the remission of sins" (Matthew 26:28).

"But if we walk in the light, as he is in the light, we have fellowship one with another, and the blood of Jesus Christ his Son cleanseth us from all sin" (1 John 1:7).

THE   BLOOD   OF   QUETZALCOATL   WAS   VERY IMPORTANT TO HIS PEOPLE.

By offering his blood, Quetzalcoatl holds the symbols of priesthood (Burland, C.A. *The Gods' of Mexico,* p. 93; see also p. 156).

4.71.   JESUS CHRIST WAS A REDEEMER FOR HIS PEOPLE.
"... God sent forth his Son, made of a woman, made under the law, To redeem them that were under the law, that we might receive the

adoption of sons" (Galatians 4:4-5; see also Job 19:25; Ephesians 1:7; Titus 2:14).

QUETZALCOATL WAS A REDEEMER FOR HIS PEOPLE.

"By the third picture (of the *Codex Fejervary-Mayer*) we have entered the era...of the age of Quetzalcoatl as redeemer" (Nicholson. *Mexican and Central American Mythology*" p. 96, see also p. 92).

4.72. EVEN THOUGH JESUS CHRIST WAS GOD, HE SUFFERED FOR HIS PEOPLE.

"Ought not Christ to have suffered these things, and to enter into his glory?"

(Luke 24:26; Acts 17:3; Hebrews 5:8 and 1 Peter 2:21).

EVEN THOUGH QUETZALCOATL WAS GOD, HE SUFFERED FOR HIS PEOPLE.

"... symbolism of the plumed serpent (Quetzalcoatl) the humble, suffering god who was brave enough to save the world from destruction when the sum stood still" (Nicholson. *Mexican and Central American Mythology*, p. 12 and 96).

4.73. JESUS CHRIST CARRIED HIS CROSS.

"... And he took Jesus, and led him away. And he bearing his cross went forth into a place called the place of a skull, which is called in the Hebrew Golgotha" (John 19:16-17).

There are six places in the New Testament where Jesus taught his disciples, "take up your cross and follow me" (Matthew 10:38; 16:24; Mark 8:34; 10:21; Luke 9:23; 14:27).

GOD OF THE POCHTECA INDIANS CARRIED HIS CROSS.

"The Pochtecas: There was also a band of followers of Quetzal-coatl...vendors who formed a guild or brotherhood...As followers of Quetzalcoatl, they were carriers of ideas as well as goods, and helped to spread the cult of the plumed serpent over a widespread area" (Nicholson. *Mexican and Central American Mythology*, pp. 92-93).

An ancient manuscript, the *Codex Fejervary-Mayer*, shows the god of the Pochtecas Indians carrying his cross. The actual name of this god was Yacatecuhtli, evidently another name for Quetzalcoatl.

See the cover of this study, in the green circle, and page iii, for further information on this interesting parallel. See also Parallel 6.25 of this study for related information.

4.74. JESUS CHRIST WAS CRUCIFIED.

The crucifixion of Jesus Christ is recorded in Matthew 27, Mark 15, Luke 23, and John 19.

QUETZALCOATL WAS CRUCIFIED.
"The Aztecs have a tradition of a God suffering and crucified named Quetzalcoatl" (Kingsborough. *Antiquities of Mexico,* Vol. 8, p. 3; see also Vol. 6, p. 166).

"... it must be regarded as a curious fact, that the Cross should have been venerated as an object of religious worship both in the New World, and in the regions of the Old, where the light of Christianity had never risen" (Prescott. *History of the Conquest of Mexico,* Vol. 1, pp. 254-255; see also pp. 219-220).

4.75. TWO PERSONS WERE CRUCIFIED WITH JESUS CHRIST.
"And they crucified him...then were there two thieves crucified with him, one on the right hand, and another on the left" (Matthew 27:35, 38).
TWO PERSONS WERE CRUCIFIED WITH QUETZALCOATL.
"In the fourth page of the Borgian Ms. he (Quetzalcoatl) seems to be crucified between two persons who are in the act of reviling him" (Kingsborough. *Antiquities of Mexico,* Vol.6, p, 166).

4.76. JESUS CHRIST LOST HIS GARMENTS BEFORE RETURNING TO HEAVEN.
"And when they had crucified him, they parted his garments, casting lots upon them, what every man should take" (Mark 15:24; John 19:23).
QUETZALCOATL LOST HIS GARMENTS BEFORE RETURNING TO HEAVEN.
"Quetzalcoatl, as a ruler on earth, also had to leave his...garments...before he could be taken into the heavens..." (Burland and Forman. *The Aztecs,* p. 46).

4.77. "PHYSICAL" DARKNESS COVERED THE EARTH WHEN JESUS CHRIST FINISHED HIS MINISTRY.
"Now from the sixth hour (when Jesus was on the cross) there was darkness over all the land unto the ninth hour" (Matthew 27:45).
"PHYSICAL" DARKNESS COVERED THE EARTH WHEN QUETZALCOATL FINISHED HIS MINISTRY.
"... at the disappearance of Topiltzin or Quetzalcoatl, both sun and moon were covered with darkness" (DeRoo. *America Before Columbus,* p. 431; Boturini. *Travels in New Spain,*1746).

4.78. **"SPIRITUAL" DARKNESS WOULD COVER THE EARTH AFTER JESUS CHRIST FINISHED HIS MINISTRY.**

"Let no man deceive you by any means: for that day (second coming of Christ) shall not come, except there come a falling away first, and that man of sin be revealed, the son of perdition" (2 Thessalonians 2:3).

"And it was given unto him (the Dragon) to make war with the saints, and to overcome them: and power was given him over all kindreds, and tongues, and nations" (Revelation 13:7).

The fact that there have became hundreds of divisions of Christian churches, each claiming to know more truth than the others, show that spiritual darkness really did occur.

"SPIRITUAL" DARKNESS WOULD COVER THE EARTH AFTER QUETZALCOATL FINISHED HIS MINISTRY.

A terrible change came upon men when Quetzalcoatl had to flee and Tezcatlipoca received power over the land (Burland, C.A. *The Gods of Mexico*, p. 141; Nicholson. *Mexican and Central American Mythology*, p. 85).

4.79. **AFTER JESUS CHRIST DIED, HE VISITED THE SPIRITS IN THE "UNDERWORLD."**

"Verily, verily, I say unto you, The hour is coming, and now is, when the dead shall hear the voice of the Son of God: and they that hear shall live" (John 5:25).

"For Christ...put to death in the flesh, but quickened by the Spirit: By which also he went and preached unto the spirits in prison which sometime were disobedient, when once the longsuffering of God waited in the days of Noah, while the ark was a preparing, wherein few, that is, eight souls were saved by water" (1 Peter 3:18-20).

"For for this cause was the gospel preached also to them that are dead, that they might be judged according to men in the flesh, but live according to God in the spirit" (1 Peter 4:6).

AFTER QUETZALCOATL DIED, HE VISITED THE SPIRITS IN THE "UNDERWORLD."

"Quetzalcoatl was said to have opened up this hole into the deepest part of the world (the underworld)" (Brundage. *The Fifth Sun*, p. 11; see also p. 123).

Traditions are abundant that Quetzalcoatl traveled into the darkness of the underworld for four (or two) days. Venus, his planet, was invisible during that time (Burland and Forman. *The Aztecs*, pp. 35-36; Burland, C.A. *The Gods of Mexico*, pp. 161 and 102; Nicholson, *Mexican and Central American Mythology*, p. 89).

4.80. JESUS CHRIST HAS BEEN RESURRECTED FROM THE DEAD.

"Fear not ye: for I know that ye seek Jesus, which was crucified. He is not here: for he is risen..." (Matthew 28:5-6; Mark 16:9 and Luke 24:39).

QUETZALCOATL HAS BEEN RESURRECTED FROM THE DEAD.

Quetzalcoatl makes his last journey, is destroyed, and then is resurrected from the grave (Burland, C.A. *The Gods of Mexico,* p. 163). The Mayans believed in the resurrection from death (Nicholson. *Mexican and Central American Mythology;* p. 21).

4.81. THE RESURRECTION OF JESUS CHRIST ALLOWED OTHER PEOPLE TO BE RESURRECTED.

When Jesus was resurrected, "... the graves were opened; and many bodies of the saints which slept arose, And came out of the graves after his resurrection, and went into the holy city, and appeared unto many" (Matthew 27:52-53; John 11:25).

THE RESURRECTION OF QUETZALCOATL ALLOWED OTHER PEOPLE TO BE RESURRECTED.

Quetzalcoatl was the god of resurrection and Tezcatlipoca was the god of death

(Nicholson. *Mexican and Central American Mythology,* pp. 95, 122 and 123; Burland and Forman, *The Aztecs,* p. 29).

4.82. JESUS CHRIST APPEARED TO HIS DISCIPLES AFTER HIS DEATH.

"... he (Jesus) through the Holy Ghost had given commandments unto the apostles whom he had chosen: To whom also he shewed himself alive after his passion by many infallible proofs, being seen of them forty days..." (Acts 1:2-3; John 20:19 and 21:1).

QUETZALCOATL APPEARED TO HIS DISCIPLES AFTER HIS DEATH.

"... the temple-sanctuary was built by the Emperor Vira-cocha to honor the god Viracocha (another name for Quetzalcoatl), who had appeared to him predicting his victory over the Chancas" (Guidoni and Magni. *The Andes,* p. 164).

4.83. JESUS CHRIST ASCENDED INTO HEAVEN AFTER HIS MISSION ON EARTH.

"...Jesus began both to do and teach, Until the day in which he was taken up..." (Acts 1:1-2).

"And when he had spoken these things, while they beheld, he was taken up; and a cloud received him out of their sight" (Acts 1:9).

QUETZALCOATL ASCENDED INTO HEAVEN AFTER HIS MISSION ON EARTH.

"Quetzalcoatl...rose to the sky and trained into the Morning Star" (Leonard. *Ancient America,* p. 59).

Quetzalcoatl was taken into the heavens and became the Morning Star (Burland and Forman. *The Aztecs,* p. 46; Burland, C.A. *The Gods of Mexico,* pp. 66 and 95).

4.84.   JESUS CHRIST PROMISED HE WOULD RETURN AGAIN AFTER HIS DEATH.

"For the Son of man shall come in the glory of his Father with his angels; and then he shall reward every man according to his works" (Matthew 16:27; Acts 1:11).

QUETZALCOATL PROMISED HE WOULD RETURN AGAIN AFTER HIS DEATH.

"The Aztecs have a tradition of a God suffering and crucified named Quetzalcoatl...He promised to return again and redeem His people" (Kingsborough. *Antiquities of Mexico,* Vol. 8, p. 3).

"Quetzalcoatl...promised, on his departure, to return at some future day with his posterity, and resume the possession of his empire" (Prescott. *History of the Conquest of Mexico,* Vol. 1, p. 289).

Quetzalcoatl's promise to return is one of most popular traditions of the native Americans.

(Burland and Forman. *The Aztecs,* p. 7; Burland, C.A. *The Gods of Mexico,* p. 147; Brundage. *The Fifth Sun,* pp. 50-51; Honore. *In Quest of the White God,* p. 16; Leonard. *Ancient America,* p. 59-60; Nicholson, *Mexican and Central American Mythology,* p. 18; Roys. *The Book of Chilam Balam of Chumayel,* p. 182; Toor. *A Treasury of Mexican Folkways,* p. xxv; Von Hagen. *The Ancient Sun Kingdoms of the Americas,* p. 193)

4.85.   JESUS CHRIST WILL RETURN FROM THE EAST.

"For as the lightning cometh out of the east, and shineth even unto the west; so shall also the coming of the Son of man be" (Matthew 24:27; Revelations 7:2).

QUETZALCOATL WILL RETURN FROM THE EAST.

"Quetzalcoatl...rose to the sky and turned into the Morning Star. But before he left he promised to return from the direction of the rising sun" (Leonard. *Ancient America,* pp. 59-60, also p. 68).

Quetzalcoatl sailed away in the east and will return from the east (Toor. *A Treasury of Mexican Folkways,* p. xxv).

4.86. WHEN JESUS CHRIST RETURNS, THERE WILL BE A RESTORATION OF THE TRUE GOSPEL.

"And he shall send Jesus Christ, which before was preached unto you: Whom the heaven must receive until the times of restitution of all things, which God hath spoken by the mouth of all his holy prophets since the world began" (Acts 3:20-21).

WHEN QUETZALCOATL RETURNS, THERE WILL BE A RESTORATION OF THE TRUE GOSPEL.

"A new wisdom shall dawn upon the world universally, in the east, north, west, and south. It shall come from the mouth of God the Father.... These are fundamentally prophecies of the return of Kukulcan, or Quetzalcoatl, Mexican culture-hero" (Roys. *The Book of Chilam Balam of Chumayel,* p.164).

"The philosophers and the higher priests knew that the power of Tezcatlipoca would come to an end in the fullness of time, only to replaced by the more complete worship of Quetzalcoatl" (Burland, C.A. *The Gods of Mexico,* p. 116).

4.87. THE ATONEMENT OF JESUS CHRIST SAVES THE UNIVERSE FROM EXTINCTION.

"For as in Adam all die, even so in Christ shall all be made alive" (1 Corinthians 15:22; John 3:14-16).

THE ATONEMENT OF QUETZALCOATL SAVES THE UNIVERSE FROM EXTINCTION.

"Quetzalcoatl...is the plumed serpent in his lowliest state, but his self-sacrifice saves the universe from extinction..." (Nicholson. *Mexican and Central American Mythology,* p. 75).

So—
**Did Jesus Christ visit ancient America?
Was he known as Quetzalcoatl?**

"And all the evidence slowly coming to light...there could be only one explanation: the Aztec myth about the White God must refer to the Messiah" (Honore. *In Quest of the White God,* p. 70).

Yes!

Section Five

Satan

Was in

Ancient America

He was known as Tezcatlipoca.

The Franciscan friar Bernardino de Sahagun was very opinionated about the identity of the many gods of ancient America. About Tezcatlipoca he said:

> "This wicked Tezcatlipoca we know is Lucifer (Satan), the great devil who there in the midst of heaven, even in the beginning, began war, vice, and filth" (Sahagun. *General History of the Things of New Spain,* 1:37).

Why did he believe such a thing? He was very close to the traditions of the American Indians, and he recognized the many similarities between the god Tezcatlipoca and Satan.

This section lends supports to his theory. The following parallels between Satan and Tezcatlipoca are quite obvious.

5.1. THE ADVERSARY OF JESUS CHRIST WAS SATAN.

"And he (Jesus) was there in the wilderness forty days, tempted of Satan; and was with wild beasts; and the angels ministered unto him" (Mark 1:13; 2 Corinthians 11:14; 2 Thessalonians 2:9 and Revelation 12:9).

THE ADVERSARY OF QUETZALCOATL WAS TEZCATLIPOCA.

"The greatest god of this group (a demiurge) is Tezcatlipoca, in myth the adversary of Quetzalcoatl" (Brundage. *The Fifth Sun,* p. 69).

Quetzalcoatl was opposed by the god Tezcatlipoca (Burland and Forman. *The Aztecs,* p. 7; Burland, C.A. *The Gods of Mexico,* pp. 36-

37; Nicholson. *Mexican and Central American Mythology,* p. 127; Toor. *A Treasury of Mexican Folkways,* p. 458; Von Hagen. *The Ancient Sun Kingdoms of the Americas,* p. 52, footnote).

5.2.   SATAN USED TO LIVE IN HEAVEN.

"How art thou fallen from heaven, O Lucifer, son of the morning!" (Isaiah 14:12) (Lucifer is Satan).

"And there was a war in heaven: Michael and his angels fought against the dragon; and the dragon fought and his angels" (Revelation 12:7-8).

TEZCATLIPOCA USED TO LIVE IN HEAVEN.

Tezcatlipoca was a fallen angel, cast down from heaven (Nicholson. *Mexican and Central American Mythology,* pp. 98, 109).

Seven devils called *satai* are from the foundation of the heavens (Makemson. *The Book of the Jaguar Priest* [*The Book of Chilam Balam of Tizimin*], p. 35).

5.3.   IN HEAVEN, SATAN COMPETED TO BECOME THE LIGHT OF THIS WORLD.

"How art thou fallen from heaven, O Lucifer, son of the morn-ing...For thou hast said in thine heart, I will ascend into heaven, I will exalt my throne above the stars of God...I will ascend above the heights of the clouds; I will be like the most High" (Isaiah 14:12-14).

IN HEAVEN, TEZCATLIPOCA COMPETED TO BECOME THE LIGHT OF THIS WORLD.

"In Aztec myth a game of *tlachtli* that changed the course of the present aeon was once played between the gods Quetzalcoatl and Tezcatlipoca. During the game, which was to decide who of the two was to be the sun..." (Brundage. *The Fifth Sun,* pp. 11-12).

5.4.   SATAN WAS CAST OUT OF HEAVEN.

"And there was a war in heaven...And the great dragon was cast out, that old serpent, called the Devil, and Satan, which deceiveth the whole world: he was cast out into the earth, and his angels were cast out with him" (Revelation 12:7-9; Isaiah 14:12-14).

TEZCATLIPOCA WAS CAST OUT OF HEAVEN.

"Then there is the myth of Tezcatlipoca's fall from heaven. Here we are told that he had sinned and, like Lucifer, was hurled down from the ambrosial regions...there may once have been a connection between Tezcatlipoca's fall from heaven and his loss of a foot and its replacement by a mirror" (Brundage. *The Fifth Sun,* p. 94, also see p. 94).

Tezcatlipoca was a fallen angel, cast down from heaven (Nicholson. *Mexican and Central American Mythology,* pp. 98, 109).

5.5. **SATAN WAS A SPIRIT AND WAS NOT BORN AS A MORTAL BEING LIKE JESUS.**

Satan enters into people (Luke 22:3; John 13:27), and he is cast out of people (Matthew 9:34). There is no record of his mortal birth, life, or death in any of the scriptures. He is universally believed to be an evil spirit.

TEZCATLIPOCA WAS A SPIRIT AND WAS NOT BORN AS A MORTAL BEING LIKE QUETZALCOATL.

Tezcatlipoca was a ruler on earth like Quetzalcoatl, except be was a non-material being, a spirit (Burland and Forman. *The Aztecs,* p. 58).

5.6. **Satan was an enemy to the plan of God.**

"And the great dragon was cast out, that old serpent, called the Devil, and Satan, which deceiveth the whole world: he was cast out into the earth, and his angels were cast out with him" (Revelation 12:9; 2 Thessalonians 2:9).

TEZCATLIPOCA WAS AN ENEMY TO THE PLAN OF GOD.

Tezcatlipoca was a wayward god with great power to control man and life away from the truth (Nicholson. *Mexican and Central American Mythology,* pp. 96 and 98).

5.7. **THE NAME OF THE CHRISTIAN "SATAN" IS VERY SIMILAR TO THE ANCIENT AMERICAN "SATAI."**

The name "Satan" appears seventeen times in the Old Testament and thirty-six times in the New Testament.

THE ANCIENT AMERICAN "SATAI."

Satai is the name of seven devils who came from heaven to create discord on earth. It probably originates from the word *zata* which means discord (Makemson. *The Book of the Jaguar Priest* [*The Book of Chilam Balam of Tizimin*], pp. 35, 36, and 157).

5.8. **SATAN HAD MANY OTHER NAMES.**

Beelzebub, Prince of the devils (Mark 3:22).

Lucifer (Isaiah 14:12).

Perdition (John 17:12).

Prince of this world (John 12:31).

The Adversary (1 Peter 5:8).

TEZCATLIPOCA HAD MANY OTHER NAMES.

Huemac, "he who is in a big hand" (Brundage. *The Fifth Sun,* p. 97).

Huitzilopochtli, "the blue hummingbird on the left" (Burland and Forman. *The Aztecs.* p. 55).

Monenequi, "he who pretends to be what he is not" (Brundage. *The Fifth Sun,* p. 90).

Satai, (Makemson. *The Book of the Jaguar Priest* [*The Book of Chilam Balam of Tizimin*], p. 35).

Smoking Mirror (Burland, C.A. *The Gods of Mexico*, p 44).

Titlauacan, "he who is at the shoulder" (Burland, C.A. *The Gods of Mexico*, p. 44).

Tlacahuepan (Brundage. *The Fifth Sun*, p. 95).

Zotz (Nicholson. *Mexican and Central American Mythology*, p. 127).

5.9.   KNOWLEDGE OF GOOD AND EVIL CAME TO EARTH BY SATAN.

"And the LORD God commanded the man, saying, Of every tree of the garden thou mayest freely eat: But of the tree of the knowledge of good and evil, thou shalt not eat of it: for in the day that thou eatest thereof thou shalt surely die...And the serpent (Satan) said unto the woman, Ye shall not surely die: For God doth know that in the day ye eat thereof, then your eyes shall be opened, and ye shall be as gods, knowing good and evil...she took the fruit thereof, and did eat, and gave also unto her husband with her; and he did eat" (Genesis 2:16-17; 3:4-6).

KNOWLEDGE OF GOOD AND EVIL CAME TO EARTH BY TEZCATLIPOCA.

"Some say that Tezcatlipoca dropped from heaven...bringing to mankind the gift of intelligence" (Nicholson. *Mexican and Central American Mythology*, p. 98).

5.10.   TWO TREES, ONE GOOD AND ONE EVIL, REPRESENTED JESUS AND SATAN.

In the garden of Eden there were two special trees. One tree was the tree of life, which fruit was to be eaten by Adam and Eve until after they partook of the other tree, the tree of knowledge of good and evil, which Satan wanted them to eat from (Genesis 2:16-17; 3:24 and 3:3-5).

TWO TREES, ONE GOOD AND ONE EVIL, REPRESENTED QUETZALCOATL AND TEZCATLIPOCA.

"Under this sky they placed two trees, surrogates for Quetzalcoatl and Tezcatlipoca..." (Brundage. *The Fifth Sun*, p. 31).

5.11.   SATAN WAS A GOD OF DARKNESS.

"For ye were sometimes darkness, but now are ye light in the Lord: walk as children of light...And have no fellowship with the unfruitful works of darkness, but rather reprove them" (Ephesians 5:8-11; 1 John 1:5-6).

"... the beast; and his kingdom was full of darkness; and they gnawed their tongues for pain" (Revelation 16:10).

TEZCATLIPOCA WAS A GOD OF DARKNESS.

"Blackness was always associated with Tezcatlipoca. To the Aztecs night time was filled with phantoms and goblins and all of these could be indiscriminately identified with Tezcatlipoca" (Brundage. *The Fifth Sun*, p. 84).

Tezcatlipoca represented shadow, darkness, smoke, clouding, black, obsidian, etc.

(Burland and Forman. *The Aztecs*, pp. 7 and 56; Burland, C.A. *The Gods of Mexico*, pp. x and 99; Nicholson. *Mexican and Central American Mythology*, p. 110).

5.12. EVEN THOUGH SATAN WAS A GOD OF DARKNESS, HE ALSO HAD THE POWER TO APPEAR AS AN ANGEL OF LIGHT.

"And no marvel; for Satan himself is transformed into an angel of light" (2 Corinthians 11:14).

EVEN THOUGH TEZCATLIPOCA WAS A GOD OF DARKNESS, HE ALSO HAD THE POWER TO APPEAR AS AN ANGEL OF LIGHT.

"Tezcatlipoca, when god of the night, disguised himself as a tiger whose spotted skin resembled the sky replete with stars. Then he transformed himself into the sun to light the world" (Toor. *A Treasury of Mexican Folkways*, p. 458).

5.13. SATAN WAS A TEMPTER AT THE SHOULDER.

"And he shewed me Joshua the high priest standing before the angel of the LORD, and Satan standing at his right hand to resist him" (Zechariah 3:1).

Many illustrations have been drawn by Hebrews and Christians showing a little red devil with a tail and a pitchfork on one shoulder and an angel on the other, one is trying to lead people to do bad, the other to do good.

TEZCATLIPOCA WAS A TEMPTER AT THE SHOULDER.

"... the ruler of power who had replaced Quetzalcoatl in the later Toltec times was Tezcatlipoca...Another of his titles, Titlauacan, means *he who is at the shoulder*, the god who, standing beside the shoulder of every human being, whispered thoughts into his mind which diverted every action towards his own direction of darkness and cruelty" (Burland, C.A. *The Gods of Mexico*, p. 44, pp. 131-132, 140).

5.14. "PRINCE OF THIS WORLD" IS A TITLE OF SATAN.

"Jesus answered and said, This voice came not because of me, but for your sakes, Now is the judgment of this world: now shall the prince of this world be cast out" (John 12:30-31, a reference to Satan).

"Hereafter I will not talk much with you: for the prince of this world cometh, and hath nothing in me" (John 14:30, 16:8-11).

"PRINCE OF THIS WORLD" IS A TITLE OF TEZCATLIPOCA.

"Tezcatlipoca: Mirror that Smokes. The Prince of this world" (Burland, C.A. *The Gods of Mexico,* p. x, see also p. 104).

5.15. SATAN WAS CALLED THE "PRINCE OR LORD OF THE AIR."

"Wherein in time past ye walked according to the course of this world, according to the prince of the power of the air, the spirit that now worketh in the children of disobedience" (Ephesians 2:2).

TEZCATLIPOCA WAS CALLED THE "PRINCE OR LORD OF THE AIR."

"Tezcatlipoca is Lord of the Air...and Tlaloc, Lord of all Waters..." (Burland, C.A. *The Gods of Mexico,* p. 78).

5.16. SATAN AND JESUS SHARED THE SYMBOL OF THE SERPENT.

"And as Moses lifted up the serpent in the wilderness, even so must the Son of man (Jesus) be lifted up" (John 3:14). Thus, the serpent of Moses represented Jesus.

Satan was represented by the serpent in the garden of Eden who convinced Adam and Eve to eat the fruit of the tree of knowledge of good and evil (Genesis 3).

TEZCATLIPOCA AND QUETZALCOATL SHARED THE SYMBOL OF THE SERPENT.

"The myth states that Quetzalcoatl and Tezcatlipoca—here cast as demiurges— assumed the form of serpents" (Brundage. *The Fifth Sun,* p. 31).

5.17. SATAN IS A GOD OF CONFUSION, HE DOES GOOD AND EVIL.

"And if Satan cast out Satan, he is divided against himself; how shall then his kingdom stand?" (Matthew 12:26).

"And no marvel; for Satan himself is transformed into an angel of light" (2 Corinthians 11:14).

TEZCATLIPOCA IS A GOD OF CONFUSION, HE DOES GOOD AND EVIL.

"Tezcatlipoca...was also called the Enemy of Both Sides, which stressed his single-minded concentration on discord itself, not on the victory of any faction. He consistently stirred up rancor so that peace should depart from cities and war should overrun the land" (Brundage. *The Fifth Sun,* p. 85).

5.18. THE DISCIPLES OF JESUS FELL INTO SPIRITUAL DARKNESS CAUSED BY SATAN.

"Let no man deceive you by any means: for that day (second coming of Christ). shall not come, except there come a falling away first, and that man of sin be revealed, the son of perdition" (2 Thessalonians 2:3).

"For the time will come when they will not endure sound doctrine..." (2 Timothy 4:3).

The "Dark Ages" of about A.D. 400-800 came to the world at a time when Christianity should have been fully developed into the "Light Ages" (Jesus was the Light of the world, See John 1:4-9), but, as predicted in the scriptures, light turned into darkness.

THE DISCIPLES OF QUETZALCOATL FELL INTO SPIRITUAL DARKNESS CAUSED BY TEZCATLIPOCA.

"The legends all agree that at the time of the last, or last but one, of the rulers of the Toltecs, the worship of Quetzalcoatl took a secondary place to that of the terrible Tezcatlipoca" (Burland, C.A. *The Gods of Mexico*, p. 37).

Quetzalcoatl's religion was transformed by the time the Spanish arrived in the New World (Nicholson. *Mexican and Central American Mythology*, p. 70).

5.19. SATAN MADE WAR WITH THE TRUTH AND TEMPORARILY RECEIVED POWER OVER ALL PEOPLE.

"And he (Satan) opened his mouth in blasphemy against God...And it was given unto him to make war with the saints, and to overcome them: and power was given him over all kindreds, and tongues, and nations. And all that dwell upon the earth shall worship him..." (Revelation 13:6-8).

"For the time will come when they will not endure sound doctrine..." (2 Timothy 4:3).

During and after the Dark Ages there appeared hundreds of separate Christian denominations, each preaching different gospels and claiming to be closer to the truth about Jesus than all the others.

TEZCATLIPOCA MADE WAR WITH THE TRUTH AND TEMPORARILY RECEIVED POWER OVER ALL PEOPLE.

In a spiritual revolution, the power of Tezcatlipoca took the place of the ruler Quetzalcoatl throughout the land of the Toltecs (Burland, C.A. *The Gods of Mexico*, p.44-45).

"... the mistaken idea that the basic religion of middle America was founded on human sacrifice and the tearing out of hearts. The human acts of blood rituals and licensed homicide came later, and were a distortion of what must once have been an extraordinarily complete vision of the place of man and of organic life in the universe...a religion of love and of consciousness became debased into a cult of the master race" (Nicholson. *Mexican and Central American Mythology*, pp. 10-11).

5.20. **IN THE LAST DAYS, JESUS WILL DESTROY SATAN AND RESTORE THE TRUTH.**

"And he shall send Jesus Christ, which before was preached unto you: Whom the heaven must receive until the times of restitution of all things, which God hath spoken by the mouth of all his holy prophets since the world began (Acts 3:21).

"That in the dispensation of the fulness of times he might gather together in one all things in Christ, both which are in heaven, and which are on earth; even in him" (Ephesians 1:10).

"And I saw another angel fly in the midst of heaven, having the everlasting gospel to preach unto them that dwell on the earth, and to every nation, and kindred, and tongue, and people...for the hour of his judgment is come..." (Revelation 14:6-7).

IN THE LAST DAYS, QUETZALCOATL WILL DESTROY TEZCATLIPOCA AND RESTORE THE TRUTH.

A future event is described thus: "The aeon itself ended only with the extinguishing of Tezcatlipoca's sun. This feat was performed by the god Quetzalcoatl, who knocked Tezcatlipoca out of the sky, whence he tumbled into the dark waters that surrounded the earth" (Brundage. *The Fifth Sun*, pp. 92-93).

When Quetzalcoatl returns the power of Tezcatlipoca would come to an end (Burland and Forman. *The Aztecs*, pp. 52, 71, and 112).

Yes—Satan was in ancient America!

Section Six

The Conclusion

Listed in this study we have the following evidences:

There are eighty-four similarities between Israelites and ancient Americans.
So—Israelites were in ancient America

There are thirty-two similarities between the Bible and the Popol Vuh;
So—Bible scriptures were in ancient America

There are fifty-three similarities between Christians and ancient Americans.
So—Christians were in ancient America

There are eighty-seven similarities between Jesus Christ and Quetzalcoatl.
So—Jesus Christ was in ancient America

There are twenty similarities between Satan and Tezcatlipoca,
So—Satan was in ancient America

**Yes—These 276 similarities prove that
The title of this study is really true!**

It is interesting and amazing that after so much good information is available to show us that Jesus did visit Israelites in ancient America, and that he taught them the true gospel—which corresponds with the Old Testament and the New Testament—yet, most Christian Churches do not believe it or even know about it.

Bibliography

Bailey, Helen Miller, and Grijalva, Maria Celia. *Fifteen Famous Latin Americans.* California: in California State Department of Education, 1973.

Bancroft, Hubert Howe. *History of Mexico.* Vol. 2. San Francisco, California: The History Company Publishers, 1886.

Bancroft, Hubert Howe. *The Native Races of the Pacific States.* Vol. 5. San Francisco, California: The History Company Publishers, 1886.

Berry, Geoge Ricker. *The Interlinear Literal Translation of The Greek-English New Testament,* and *Greek-English New Testament Lexicon.* 15th ed. Grand Rapids, Michigan: Zondervan Publishing House, 1974.

Boturini, Chevalier. *Travels in New Spain.* America, 1746.

Brinton, D.G. *Myths of the New World.* Philadelphia, Pennsylvania: David McKay, 1868.

Brundage, Burr Cartwright. *The Fifth Sun, Aztec Gods, Aztec World.* Austin, Texas: University of Texas Press, 1979.

Burland, C.A. *The Gods of Mexico.* New York: G.P. Putnam's Sons, 1967.

Burland, Cottie, and Forman, Werner. *The Aztecs.* New York: Galahad Books, 1975.

Carrasco, David. *Religions of Mesoamerica.* New York: Harper and Roe Publishers, 1990.

Colton, Calvin. *Origin of the American Indians.* London, England, 1833.

DeRoo, P. *History of America before Columbus.* Philadelphia, Pennsylvania: Lippincott, 1900.

Ebersheim. *The Life and Times of Jesus the Messiah.* Vol. 2. 1883.

Farrar, Fredrick W. *The Life of Christ.* London, England: Cassell and Company Limited, 1874; Salt Lake City, Utah: Bookcraft, 1998.

Fell, Barry. *America B.C.* New York: The New York Times Book Company, 1976.

Funk and Wagnalls New EncyclopediaI Vol. 8, 12, 13 and 20. USA: Rand McNally et al., 1961.

Glaser, Lynn. *Indians or Jews?* California: Roy V. Boswell Gilroy, 1973.

Goetz and Morley. *Popol Vuh, The Sacred Book of the Ancient Quiche Maya.* English version by Goetz and Sylvanus G. Morley from the translation of Adrian Recinos. University of Oklahoma Press, 1950.

Guidoni, Enrico, and Magni, Roberto. *Monuments of Civilization—The Andes.* New York: Grosset and Dunlap Inc., 1977.

Halley, Henry H. *Halley's Bible Handbook.* 24th ed. Grand Rapids, Michigan: Zondervan Publishing House, 1965.

Herrmann, Paul. *Conquest by Man.* New York: Harper, 1954.

Honore, Pierre. *In Quest of the White God.* New York: G.P. Putnam's Sons, 1964.

Israel, Manasseh ben. *The Hope of Israel.* London, England: R.I. for Livewell Chapman, 1652.

Whiston, William, and Nimmo, William P. *Josephus Complete Works.* Standard ed. Philadelphia: Porter and Coates, 1867.

Kelly, David H. "Calendar Animals and Deities," *Southwestern Journal of Anthropology.* 1960.

Kingsborough, Lord. *Antiquities of Mexico.* Vol. 9. England: Henry G. Bohn, 1830-1848.

Lee, J. Fitzgerald. *The Great Migration.* 1932.

Leonard, Jonathan Norton. *Ancient America.* Reprinted for the Time-Life Books, John D. Manley, 1975.

Lund, Nils Wilhelm. *Chiasmus in the New Testament.* Chapel Hill:University of North Carolina Press, 1942. Peabody, Massachusetts: Hendrickson Publishers, Inc., 1992.

Makemson, Maud Worcester. *The Book of The Jaguar Priest,* an English translation of *The Book of Chilam Balam of Tizimin,* with commentary. New York: H. Wolfe Book Manufacturing Co., 1951.

National Geographic Society. *National Parks of North America.* The Book Division of the National Geographic Society, 1995.

Newsweek Books. *Milestones of History, Ancient Empires.* New York, 1973.

Nicholson, Irene. *Mexican And Central American Mythology.* England: The Hamlyn Publishing Group Limited, 1967.

Poindexter, Miles. *The Ayar-Incas,* Vol. 2. New York: H. Liveright, 1930.

Prescott, William H. *History of the Conquest of Mexico.* Vol.1. Philadelphia: David McKay, 1891; Vol. 2. Boston, Massachusetts: Phillips, Sampson and Company, 1856.

Roys, Ralph L. *The Book of Chilam Balam of Chumayel.* Norman, Oklahoma: University of Oklahoma Press, 1967.

Smith, Rev. Ethan. *View of the Hebrews: or, the Tribes of Israel in America.* 2nd ed. Poultney, Vermont: Smith and Shute, 1825.

Smith, William. *Smith's Bible Dictionary.* 9th ed. New York: Pyramid Publications, 1974.

Thorowgood, Rev. Thomas. *Jews in America.* London, England , 1650.

Toor, Frances. *A Treasury of Mexican Folkways*. New York: Crown Publishers, 1947.

Von Hagen, Victor Wolfgang. *The Ancient Sun Kingdoms of the Americas*. Cleveland, Ohio: World Publishing Company, 1961.

Von Hagen, Victor Wolfgang. *World of the Maya*. New York: Mentor Bood by The New American Library, Inc., 1960.

Willard, T.A. *The City of the Sacred Well*. New York: The Century Co., 1926.

Topical Index

Israel - 1.23.
Irac Baskets - 1.66.
Israelite Scriptures - Section Two.
Israelites - Section One.

Jacob - 1.22.
Jesus - 3.17, 3.37, Section Four, 5.1, 5.16, 5.18, 5.20.
Jews - 1.41, 1.43, 1.81.

King of the Earth - 4.45.
Kukulkan - 1.46, 3.35, 4.13, 4.16, 4.86.

Ladder from Heaven to Earth - 1.15.
Light of the World - 4.50.
Lord Title - 4.48, 4.49
Love one another - 4.56.
Lucifer - 1.3, 2.17.

Man can become Divine - 3.33.
Man was Created - 2.14, 2.15, 2.16.
Marriage Ceremonies - 1.74, 2.25, 3.39.
Mediator - 4.61.
Mediterranean Writings - 1.56.
Melchizedek - 1.20.
Messiah Title - 4.52.
Mexico - 1.32, 1.38, 3.17.
Miriam and Chimalman - 1.30.
Missionaries - 4.44.
Mummification - 1.62.

Nicknames - 1.82, 3.51.
Noah - 1.8, 1.9, 1.10.

Objections to this Study - pages vi, vii, viii, ix.
One Supreme God - 1.1, 3.1.
Opposition in all Things - 1.55.

Papyrus Boats - 1.63.
Pentateuch of Moses - 1.16, 2.27.
Polygamy - 1.51

Popol Vuh - Section Two.
Prayer - 1.80.
Premortal Life - 1.4, 3.4.
Priesthood of God - 1.18, 1.19, 3.9, 3.19, 4.62

* * * Jesus Christ Visited Ancient America * * *

The following information is common knowledge among all Christians because it is recorded in the New Testament of the Bible.

During New Testament times, the twelve tribes of Israel were scattered over a wide area outside of Palestine.

"JAMES...to the twelve tribes which are scattered abroad..." (James 1:1).

After his resurrection, Jesus visited and taught the Israelites in and around Jerusalem for forty days.

"... HE showed himself alive after his passion by many infallible proofs, being seen of them forty days," (Acts 1:3).

Jesus would visit tribes of Israel which were scattered abroad.

"...And *other sheep I have*, which are *not of this fold*: them also I must bring, and *they shall hear my voice*..." (John 10:14-16).

This study shows that Israelites were in Ancient America, that they practiced Christianity which was taught to them by Jesus himself. **There are 276 similarities to prove this is true.**

* * * Almon Fackrell * * *

The author of this study was born in Pingree, Idaho and raised in Arimo, Idaho. In 1953 he was drafted into the U.S. Army and was assigned to a Special Weapons Detachment in New Mexico at Sandia Base, Holloman Air Force Base and White Sands Proving Grounds.

He attended the University of New Mexico and graduated at Sandia Corporation Engineering Trade School in Albuquerque.

After thirty-seven years of Drafting, Designing and Engineering in the Aerospace Industry, he retired as a Senior Support Engineer from Parker Hannifin Corporation in Irvine, California.